# THE
# WORD MADE
# FLESH

# THE WORD MADE FLESH

A Christ-Centered
Study of the
Book of John

A.B. SIMPSON

CHRISTIAN PUBLICATIONS
CAMP HILL, PENNSYLVANIA

Christian Publications
3825 Hartzdale Drive, Camp Hill, PA 17011

*Faithful, biblical publishing since 1883*

ISBN: 0-87509-577-1
© 1995 by Christian Publications
All rights reserved
Printed in the United States of America

95 96 97 98 99  5  4  3  2  1

All Scripture is taken from the Authorized
King James Version

# CONTENTS

# THE AUTHORSHIP
# OF THE
# GOSPEL OF JOHN

The most abundant internal evidence, and the testimony of the earliest witnesses among the apostolic fathers, including such names as Clement, Polycarp, Papias, Theophilus, Athenagoras, Apollinaris, Tatian, Justin Martyr, and many of the leading heretics of the early centuries besides, leave no reasonable ground to doubt that the fourth gospel was accepted from the earliest period as the work of John, the beloved disciple. Early tradition represents it as written at the request of his brethren and friends in Ephesus for the purpose of meeting the errors which were springing up in the Church at the close of the first century, by the personal testimony of the one who best knew the Lord's life and teachings. Through the influence of Philo and the Alexandrian school of Jewish and Hellenistic philosophy, many subtle errors were already pervading the minds even of Christians, and the seeds of the Gnostic heresy were widely sown, embodying, among other false teachings, the idea that the Logos, or Word, was a being inferior to God, and that the Creator of the world was really the enemy both of God and man. There was but one voice that could give an authoritative answer to all these opinions, and he was still alive as the bishop and father of the church at Ephesus; and a tradition referred to by many of the fathers, and mentioned by Eusebius as reliable, represents his brethren as waiting upon the venerable apostle and requesting him to put in permanent form his oral testimony concerning Christ. The apostle asked them to spend three days in fasting and prayer, and at the end of that time he was so filled with the Holy Spirit that he was impelled to indite the opening words of the gospel.

Clement of Alexandria says, "St. John, the last of the evangelists, when he saw that the outward bodily facts had been set forth in the existing gospels, impelled by his friends and divinely moved by the Spirit, made a spiritual gospel."

Of the personality of the author himself, we know that he was the son of Zebedee and Salome. His mother was probably the sister of Mary, the mother of the Lord, so that he was His cousin. He was, most probably, younger than the Lord or any of the apostles. His father was a fisherman, residing, it would seem, at Bethsaida and in comfortable circumstances. We read of hired servants in the household, and of Salome as one of the women who ministered to Christ of their substance. We find John himself possessing a home, to which he took the mother of the Lord as his abiding guest.

A disciple first of John the Baptist, he was also one of the first to receive his testimony concerning Christ, and immediately followed the new Master. The name which he and his brother received was Boanerges, or sons of thunder, which may have referred to his natural temperament, or, perhaps, to his spiritual fervor; thunder signifying, in the Hebrew idiom, the voice of God. His writings certainly express intense prophetic fire. The incident of his and his mother's request that he should be one of the favorites of Christ on His kingly throne, despite all its obvious touches of earthly ambition, was really prompted by the passionate love which desired to be near Him. Even the cross could not separate the ardent disciple from the Master's side (John 19:25–27). On the mount, in the death chamber at Capernaum and in the garden he was one of the three companions of the Lord's most sacred hours of service, glory and suffering, and at the table he was nearest to the bosom of Jesus. His place was recognized by all his brethren, and when the most delicate question of their life was to be whispered in the ear of the Lord, it was "the disciple whom Jesus loved, . . . reclining next to him" (13:23), that was entrusted with the task. He was the first to believe in the resurrection of Jesus (20:8), and the first to recognize his risen Lord on the shores of Galilee (21:7).

In the early apostolic ministry, we find him associated with Peter in the first miracle at Jerusalem (Acts 3) and in the suffering, persecution and testimony that followed (Acts 4). Next we find him at Samaria associated with Peter, still in apostolic labors (8:14), and at the time of Paul's second visit to Jerusalem he is mentioned by that apostle as one of the pillars of the church (Galatians 2:9).

The next reference to him in the Scriptures is in the opening of the Apocalypse many years later, where we find him on the Isle of Patmos for "the word of God and the testimony of Jesus" (Revelation 1:9). Many well-authenticated legends and traditions fill up the traditional portrait. One represents him as pursuing a youth who had wandered from the Lord, constraining him, as he threw his arms about him, to come back to the fold of Jesus. Another, as flying from the bathroom in Ephesus because he found that Cerinthus, the heretic, was within, fearing that it would fall upon him if he entered. The third describes him as carried in his old age from Sabbath to Sabbath into the church at Ephesus and repeating week after week the simple and single message, "Little children, love one another," and when asked by the fathers why he did so, replying, "It is the Lord's command, and if this alone be done, it is enough."

And a yet more singular legend, referring to Christ's words to Peter, "If I want him to remain alive until I return, what is that to you?" (John 21:22), represents it as the widely prevalent belief that John was not really dead, but was sleeping in his tomb till Christ's second coming. It was even said that "he showed that he was alive by the movement of the dust which was stirred by the breath of the saint." Even Augustine himself, in the fourth century, refers to this tradition as one that was believed in his own day by credible persons. Without requiring us to believe this curious tradition, it is enough for us to know that John did undoubtedly tarry until after the destruction of Jerusalem, which was, in some sense, the coming of the Lord to bring an immediate crisis in the Jewish dispensation. To him, also, the Master literally came, on the Isle of Patmos, to bring the vision of the coming centuries, and the panorama of His glorious coming at the end of the age. The character of John was marked by simplicity, fervor and intense spirituality. His nature was most childlike, and, therefore, most in sympathy with the divine. To trust, to love, to know were much easier for him than for natures like Peter and Thomas. Above all others, he is the apostle of love.

## OUTLINE OF THE GOSPEL OF JOHN

True to this great design to unfold the person and glory of Jesus as the Messiah and Son of God, this central thought may be traced through the whole gospel.

1. The Primeval Glory of Jesus with the Father (1:1–2).

2. His Manifest Glory in Creation, the Old Testament, and His Incarnation (1:3–14).

3. His Glory as Witnessed by His Friends and Early Followers (1:15–4:54).

a. The testimony of John the Baptist to the priests and Levites who came to inquire concerning Christ (1:15–28).

b. The revelation of Jesus to the first disciples and their acceptance of Him (1:29–51).

c. The revelation of His glory in the first miracle and the faith of the disciples in consequence (2:1–11).

d. The cleansing of the temple, the other miracles in Jerusalem and the faith of the people in consequence (2:13–25).

e. The interview with Nicodemus, representing the higher classes in Jerusalem, and their awakening interest in Him and His teachings (3:1–21).

f. The ministry in Judea, and the numerous disciples who followed Jesus and were baptized by His disciples (3:22–4:3).

g. The ministry in Samaria and the first Samaritan converts (4:4–42).

h. The successful commencement of His later ministry in Galilee and favorable reception by the Galileans, and the faith of the nobleman at Capernaum (4:43–54).

## 4. His Glory Manifested in Conflict with the Unbelief and Opposition of His Enemies (5:1–12:50).

The scene now changes and the whole section is a record of conflict ending at last in the victory of Christ over His adversaries, but a victory which cost Him His life.

a. The beginning of the conflict in Jerusalem through the healing of the invalid man at the pool of Bethesda (5:1–47).

Jesus is revealed as the source of life and rejected.

b. Decisive close of the conflict in Galilee after the discourse in the synagogue at Capernaum during the feast of the Passover (6:1–71).

Jesus, the Living Bread, is rejected by the Galileans (6:66).

c. Renewal of the conflict in Jerusalem at the Feast of Tabernacles (7:1–53).

Jesus, the Living Water, is rejected.

d. Continuance of the conflict in Jerusalem (8:12; 9:41).

Jesus is the Light of the World, as shown in the healing of the blind man, but is rejected by them in their blindness (9:41).

e. Next stage of the conflict: the Feast of Dedication in Jerusalem three months later (10:1–40).

Jesus, the Good Shepherd, is rejected, with a murderous attempt to take His life.

f. Final stage of the conflict: resurrection of Lazarus, demonstrating His divinity as beyond dispute, and determining them in their mad and malignant purpose to destroy Him.

Jesus is shown as the One who raises the dead (11:1–57).

g. Triumphal entry into Jerusalem—Jesus, the King of the Jews (12:1–50).

Christ's public acknowledgment of triumph is accepted by Him as the final challenge and leads to the final accomplishment of their purpose to destroy Him.

In this closing section the plot deepens with His triumph. The dark shadow of the betrayer falls upon the scene. Mary anoints His body in anticipation of His burial, and Christ Himself predicts His own approaching death under the figure of the kernel of wheat planted in the ground.

## 5. His Glory Manifested in His Closing Messages to His Own Disciples (13:1–17:26).

These parting words might be divided into four sections:

a. At the Passover table (chapter 13).

b. At the Lord's Supper (chapter 14).

c. On the way from the upper room through the temple (chapters 15, 16).

d. Concluding prayer, in which He speaks not to them, but of them to the Father (chapter 17).

These sublime discourses will be found more fully analyzed elsewhere.

## 6. His Glory Manifested in His Trial and Crucifixion (chapters 18, 19).

a. His arrest and the perfect voluntariness of His submission (18:1–12).

b. His trial before the Jewish council and His holy dignity in the face of their helplessness (18:13–27).

c. His trial before Pilate and His vindication by the governor as innocent (18:28–19:22).

d. His suffering and death with all the incidents which manifested forth His victorious patience, meekness and love, and the fulfillment of Scripture in every act, closing with His shout of triumph, "It is finished" (19:23–37).

e. Finally, His honorable burial through the intercession of Nicodemus and Joseph, according to the prophetic Scriptures, in the tomb of the wealthy councilor (19:38–42).

## 7. His Resurrection Glory (chapters 20, 21).

a. Witnessed by Peter and John (20:1–10).

b. Witnessed by Mary Magdalene (20:11–18).

c. Witnessed by the 11 disciples (20:19–23).

d. Witnessed by Thomas (20:24–29).

e. Witnessed by many other signs (20:30–31).

f. Manifestation of Christ's glory at the Sea of Tiberias, restoration of Peter, and prophecy concerning John (21:1–25).

g. Final testimony of John (21:24–25).

# CHAPTER I

## SCOPE AND CHARACTERISTICS OF THE GOSPEL OF JOHN

### I. ITS TEXT AND THEME

THE apostle himself expressed his special object in writing this Gospel.

"These are written, that ye might believe that Jesus is the Christ, the Son of God; and that believing ye might have life through his name" (20:31).

First, then, we may expect in it a revelation of Jesus in His twofold character as Christ and the Son of God. It is not so much a record of the facts of His life, although based upon them and presenting many new facts of great importance as a revelation of His divine and Messianic character, as it is the summing up of the testimony concerning Him that would be likely to produce a conviction of His divinity in the minds of men. And even more than all these testimonies, it is an unfolding of His higher nature from the Lord's own consciousness as expressed in His wonderful discourses, and as apprehended by the love and instinct of John and reproduced in these pages as a heart-picture of his Master's inmost life and being.

Next, we may expect, along with this, a revelation of "life through his name" as the blessed experience of those knowing and believing on Jesus as the Christ and the Son of God.

This word, *life*, is perhaps the most prominent keynote both in the Gospel and Epistles of John. Christ is the life. Salvation is life.

7

Not our acts, nor even ideas, are recognized in these pages as constituting our highest self, but that new and divine *life* which we receive from Jesus Christ through the Holy Ghost in our spirits which He imparts even to our bodies from His own risen and glorified humanity and which is to be consummated in the perfected physical and spiritual life of the resurrection. The two great themes, therefore, in John are, *Jesus Himself the Son of God* and *Life through His name.*

## 2. STYLE

The style is direct and personal, and the pictures he gives are evidently those of an eyewitness. He speaks of persons, places and incidents with the precision of vividness. Notice, for example, his reference to Cana of Galilee, Bethany beyond Jordan, Ephraim near the wilderness; the city of Samaria, called Sychar; the allusions to the temple and its feasts; the treasury, Solomon's porch and the custom of pouring out water and lighting the lamps in the temple courts at the time of the feasts. Notice also the explicit reference to details of conversations, titles, etc., as in the picture of the calling of the first disciples (chapter 1); the conversation with Philip about the bread (6:5) and the conversation of Philip and Andrew about the Greeks who came to see Jesus (12:20-22); the coming of Nicodemus by night; the vivid picture of the interview at Sychar with the woman of Samaria, the very hour of the interview with the woman and of the healing of the nobleman's son (4:6, 52); the six water pots (2:6); the five loaves and two fishes (6:9); the 38 years of sickness (5:5); the pool of Bethesda with its exact location by the Sheep gate (5:2); the pool of Siloam, with its interpretation, "Sent" (9:7); the place of the skull called Golgotha (19:17); and the Pavement or raised platform in the hall of Judgment named Gabbatha (19:13). All these and many other such allusions reveal the hand and presence of a personal witness and a direct observer, and all the scenes and incidents move before us like a living scene.

## 3. INCIDENTAL

Although the Gospel of John is the most didactic and spiritual of all the Gospels, yet all the discourses in it grow out of living facts and incidents and are vividly connected with them in the mind and picture. Even the testimony of John in the first chapter rises out of the disputations of priests and Levites. The profound discourse of the third chapter, concerning the new birth, is vivified by the midnight scene and the interesting conversation with Nicodemus. The abstruse address of the fifth chapter grows out of the healing of the impotent man. The sixth chapter is enlivened by the constant allusion, both to the recent miracle of the multiplied bread and also to the Passover now being observed at Jerusalem. The sublimest utterances of the seventh chapter are directly called forth by the striking ceremonies of the Feast of Tabernacles going on at the time. His discourse on the light of the world (chapters 8 and 9) is illumined by the figure of the suspended lamps in the court of the temple and illustrated by the healing of the blind man in Jerusalem. The picture of the Good Shepherd (in chapter 10) grows out of false shepherds just given in chapter 9. The profound address of His approaching death (chapter 12) is suggested by the previous resurrection of Lazarus and the incident of the coming of certain Greeks. In chapter 13 He teaches His disciples love; first, by washing their feet, and secondly, by interpreting and crystallizing the act in the new commandment which He gives them. The address of chapter 15 grows out of their passing the temple vine, or the vineyards by the wayside. The parting lessons of service, which He gives to Simon Peter and the other disciples, are suggested and emphasized by the beautiful miracle of the draught of fishes (chapter 21). Thus the entire Gospel is a living panorama as well as a divine oratorio.

## 4. PERSONALTY

Personal character is very vivid in the Gospel of John. More than any other of the Gospels it is a portraiture of persons, and the pictures stand out with graphic distinctness and strongly marked individuality.

First, we have the picture of the Baptist himself, and his unselfish and lofty testimony to Christ, even at the loss of his own disciples. Then follow the vivid sketches of Andrew, John, Simon, Philip and Nathaniel. Nowhere do we get the personal view of

Andrew, Philip and Nathaniel which we find in this Gospel.

The marriage scene at Cana brings out the personality of Jesus' mother and her relation to Christ.

In the strongest light the portrait of Nicodemus is drawn, and the woman of Samaria stands before us like a photograph. We can see not only her figure as she stands with her empty water-pot but can also read her very heart in the strong light of the Master's searching glance.

The nobleman of Capernaum (in chapter 4), the impotent man at Bethesda (in chapter 5) and the blind man (in chapter 9) are unmistakable in their personality.

How different Martha seems in this Gospel from the picture in Luke, as we see her bravely struggle up to the faith which should claim her brother's resurrection. How lifelike the tears of Mary as they mingle with the Master's, and how real the scene as she poured out her grateful love in the anointing at Bethany, under-standing alone of all His friends the meaning of His approaching death.

What an awful picture chapter 13 gives us of the betrayer, as he goes out in the night with the fearful words ringing in his ears, "That thou doest, do quickly" (verse 27).

How the character of Nicodemus grows, until the timid in-quirer has become the bold confessor.

How strongly marked the personality of Christ's enemies, Caiaphas even predicting His death, and the Pharisees using His inspired words to justify their malignant hate and murder.

What a look into Peter's heart John has given us, and what an awful shadow rests upon that judgment hall as Jesus looks down into Pilate's soul and bears witness to him while the message comes from his very wife which deepens his superstitious fear as the Roman governor becomes the real criminal before the power of his conscience and his Lord.

What can equal the garden scene where Mary Magdalene meets her risen Lord and the love of the Master and the disciple expresses itself in two brief words of mutual recognition, "Mary," "Rabboni" (20:16).

And how full of vividness and instructiveness are the touches which from time to time reveal to us the ardent but despondent heart of Thomas until at last the picture culminates in the resurrection scene, unfolding to us exquisitely the workings of unbelief, the triumph of faith and the marvelous grace, as well as the unmistakable reality of the risen Christ.

The last two pictures of Simon and his restoration and John himself are exquisite. We see John's modest yet bold and childlike love, nestled on the bosom of Jesus, yet nameless in his own Gospel. He is lost in the love of Jesus like the beautiful painting of Raphael, entitled "John on Jesus' Breast," where we see a head buried on the bosom of Jesus but the face is unseen, while over it there bends the tender and glowing countenance of his loving Lord.

## 5. SYMBOLISM

Throughout the entire Gospel we have a succession of impressive symbols, most of them drawn from the Old Testament. The Tabernacle becomes the type of the incarnate Christ. "The Word was made flesh, and dwelt among us" (1:14).

The lamb of the Passover becomes the figure of "the Lamb of God, which taketh away the sin of the world" (1:29).

The descending dove represents the Holy Ghost (1:32).

The ladder of Jacob shines out in full Messianic meaning in the words of Jesus to Nathaniel (1:51).

The marriage scene at Cana points forward to the whole purpose of Christ's coming and suggests the glorious figure which John plainly brings out (3:29) as the anticipation of the Marriage of the Lamb.

The temple becomes the type of His body and of His Church (2:19).

The water of Sychar's well suggests the fountain of salvation (4:14).

The harvest fields of Samaria summon to spiritual work and its glorious recompense (4:35-38).

The feeding of the five thousand (6:1-13) suggests the ancient symbol of manna and both lead on to the higher teaching of Himself as our living bread.

The waters of Siloam, as they are poured out upon the altar, suggest the smitten Rock of Horeb. Both are applied by the Lord to the living water which they that believe in Him shall receive and be able to give to others as rivers of living water (7:37-38).

The temple lamps recall the pillar of cloud and fire and are used to proclaim the glory of Jesus as the true light of the world (8:12).

The ancient figure of the shepherd is adopted by the Lord and applied to Himself and His flock (chapter 10).

The corn of wheat becomes the parable of death and resurrection in relation to Jesus and His disciples (12:24-26).

The washing of the disciples' feet may be an allusion to the ancient laver; but, at least, it becomes a symbol of spiritual cleansing (chapter 13).

The golden vine carved on the temple gate, or, perhaps, the vineyards around Jerusalem, set forth the deep spiritual teachings of the Christ-life (chapter 15).

The familiar Old Testament figure of a travailing woman illustrates the birth-throes of the new dispensation (16:21).

And the figure of the shepherd is repeated in the closing chapter and transferred from the chief Shepherd to the apostolic ministry as the Master commits the care of His little flock to His disciples.

Thus the entire Gospel is alive with shining emblems, unfolding the glory and the grace of Jesus in the light, both of nature and of Scripture. All things in earth and heaven are made tributary to the revelation of Jesus.

Someone has described a drinking fountain in Germany where every morning or noon the villagers throng to enjoy the flowing water as it pours through numerous statues, the figures representing all the forms of human life. The farmer drinks from the fountain adorned with figures of waving grain from which are traced the words, "I am the bread of life." The shepherd comes up and drinks from the outstretched hands of a shepherd holding a lamb in his bosom, and exclaims, "I am the good shepherd." The traveler sees a guide holding a lamp in his hand, as he cries, "I am the light of the world." The gardener drinks from a fountain where the waters seem to be crushed from the clusters of the grapes that hang above it in the stone almost hiding the letters, "I am the true vine." The whole realm of nature is represented and each object proclaims in its own tongue the glory and grace of Jesus while the water which they all drink speaks loudest of all, "If any man thirst, let him come unto Me and drink." So this beautiful Gospel speaks to man, not only in the tenderest words of human language, the most exquisite figures of human life and the most profound discourses of human thought, but it lays under tribute every figure of Hebrew history and the natural world as an alphabet to express in the glowing language of symbol and type the abundant grace of Him who is the First and the Last, both in nature, revelation and His people's hearts and lives.

## 6. CHRONOLOGICAL ORDER

While not a detailed narrative of Christ's life, yet the Gospel of John contains a more exact and complete reference to the leading chronological periods of Christ's life than any of the others. In perfect succession, it refers to each of the great sections of His life which we have already outlined. This will be seen by the following brief summary.

a. The inauguration of Christ's ministry is covered by the first chapter of his Gospel containing the testimony of John and the calling of the first disciples immediately after His baptism.

b. His early Galilean ministry is covered by the second chapter, giving the account of the miracle in Cana and Galilee.

c. His early Judean ministry is sketched in the early part of the second and the whole of the third, extending to the third verse of the fourth chapter.

d. His later Galilean ministry, including the journey through Samaria, falls within the fourth, fifth and sixth chapters, containing an account of a brief visit to Jerusalem made during this period.

e. His later Judean ministry includes chapters 7 to 11.

f. The last week of His ministry falls in chapter 12, closing with the five chapters which contain His final discourses, 13 to 17.

g. The last day of His life, with His trial and crucifixion, is described in chapters 18 and 19; and the story of His resurrection, as we have already seen, is covered in chapters 20 to 21.

## 7. SPIRITUAL ORDER

We find a gradual progress in the revelation of the truth in this book. The earlier chapters deal with the more fundamental doctrines and experiences of the Christian life. The sixth chapter begins with the unfolding of deeper and higher revelations of Christ, continued to the end of His discourses with the twelve at the supper table. Then comes the mystery of His death and the glory of His resurrection.

It has been compared to the approach to God's ancient temple, or tabernacle, to which, indeed, the opening verses distinctly allude in speaking of Christ. "The Word was made flesh, and dwelt among us" (1:14). "The glory as of the only begotten of the Father," referred to in the same verse, might be compared to the cloud that overshadowed the ancient tabernacle.

The first five chapters remind us of the court of the tabernacle with the altar and laver of cleansing. To the former, John the Baptist points as the Christ, "Behold the Lamb of God, which taketh away the sin of the world" (1:29). To the latter, there is a very natural allusion in the cleansing of the temple in the second chapter and the discourse with Nicodemus in the third, concerning the denial; while the fourth and fifth chapters still more freely unfold the freeness and fullness of the great salvation of which that was the type.

In the sixth chapter, we enter the next chamber, the Holy Place, where stood the table of shewbread, the lamps of gold and the altar of incense. The discourse about the living bread might well represent the first (chapter 6). The great discourse about the light of the world (chapters 8 and 9) seems almost to allude to the golden candlestick. The door (chapter 10) and abundant pasture suggest the meaning of this sacred chamber as the place of priestly access and blessing; while the altar of incense, with its hallowed teachings about communion and intercession, is appropriately suggested by the parting discourses around the communion table.     Then comes the sublime intercessory prayer of John 17 in which the great High Priest already stands at the heavenly altar, almost within the veil, and announces that blessed ministry of prayer of which the ancient altar was the type. Then the veil is rent asunder on the cross through His rent flesh, and the story of the resurrection admits us to the very Holy of Holies. He has entered in and left the way open for that blessed communion with His risen glorified person of which the closing chapters give us such beautiful examples.

### 8. REFERENCES TO OTHER SCRIPTURES

There are many striking allusions to other portions of the Bible. The opening words irresistibly suggest the first sentences of the book of Genesis. His words to Nathaniel allude to the vision of Jacob at Bethel, and His discourses to the Pharisees in Galilee and Jerusalem are crowded with references to the Old Testament—especially the three ancient saints who represented the successive periods of God's dealings with His people, namely, Abraham, Moses and Isaiah (8:56; 3:14; 12:38).

Other references to the Old Testament will be found in 2:17; 6:45; 7:38; 10:34; 12:14; 13:18; 15:25; 17:12 and 19:24, 36, 37.

There is a still closer resemblance between the Gospel of John and the Epistle of John. In both we find repeatedly the words life, light, love and others that we have found especially prominent in the Gospel. It has been strikingly said that the Epistle is an unfolding rather of the humanity and the Gospel of the divinity of Jesus. The burden of the Gospel is, Jesus is the Christ; of the Epistle, Christ is Jesus. The Epistle of John deals more directly with the errors of John's own time; the Gospel, with the conflicts of Christ's life and surroundings. There is a progress, also, in the Epistle towards the personal coming of the Lord which we find more fully developed in the Apocalypse.

The relation of John's Gospel to the other Gospels is also marked and instructive. It repeats few of the facts and discourses which they contain, showing that it is supplementary. There is no real contradiction, and there are many wonderful coincidences.

The relation of John's Gospel to the Apocalypse may be summed up in this single sentence: The Gospel describes the coming of Jesus in its spiritual and personal aspect, chiefly as His coming to the heart; the Apocalypse unfolds His literal coming to the world, His personal second advent.

The same expressions occur repeatedly in both. We have the

"Word of God," the "Lamb of God," the "Beginning of the creation of God," the "Holy Spirit" and the phraseology of cleansing and salvation.

CHAPTER 2

# JESUS THE SON
# OF GOD

WE have already seen that the Gospels of Matthew, Mark and Luke, respectively, present the picture of Christ as the King, the Servant and the Son of Man. True to the special symbol of the four Gospels, the soaring eagle represents the Master in His highest aspect as the Son of God.

No other was fitted so well to unveil the inmost heart and unfold the divine glory of the Master as he who had leaned on His bosom until he had felt the very throbbings of His heart. Both in his Gospel and in his Epistles, we have the very loftiest revealings of the character of Jesus and the profoundest spiritual truth. It is the heart that best beholds God, and love is the true element of vision. "He that loveth not knoweth not God; for God is love" (1 John 4:8). Hence, John, the apostle of love, was especially enabled to know and reveal the Son of God.

## SECTION 1—THE ETERNAL WORD (John 1:1-2)

Four great truths are here taught respecting the primeval glory of Jesus.

### 1. INDIVIDUALITY

First, His distinct personality. The Greek word, translated "the same" in the second verse, literally means "He Himself," and is the strongest distinctive expression in that language. The same strong idea of personality is expressed in the words, twice repeated, "with God." Even before His incarnation, nay, even before there was any creature in the universe, He was a living person, distinct from, and yet, one with the eternal Father. These passages completely contradict the heretical view of the Trinity entertained by some that the divine persons are just various aspects of God. In this passage, the Father and the Son are both represented as distinct individuals, as much as any being can be.

## 2. DEITY

"The Word was God" (John 1:1). The Word possesses all the attributes that God possesses. The ordinary form of expression is more forcible than it is possible to represent in the translation of the Greek tense. The imperfect expresses, as far as human language can, "the notion of absolute existence." This is the great fundamental truth which the Gospel of John develops and unfolds. He simply states it here and afterwards bears witness to it. Still stronger, if possible, is his statement in the closing words of his Epistle, "This is the true God, and eternal life" (1 John 5:20).

## 3. ETERNITY

"In the beginning" (John 1:1). This expression reverts back to Genesis 1:1. There it means the moment when the created universe came into existence. At this moment John declares Jesus Christ already was, and, therefore, had been in the previous eternity before any created existence had come into being. It implies His preexistence. This is the truth which the apostle Paul expresses so forcibly in Colossians 1:17: "He is before all things," and again, "The firstborn of every creation" (verse 15), literally, "born before the whole creation."

## 4. THE WORD

His relation to the Father, as the Image and Revealer of God. This is expressed by the term "the Word." The Greek term, *Logos,* was a familiar word in philosophical discussion in the days of John both as understood in these discussions and as the word itself naturally means. It fittingly expresses the truth that Jesus Christ is the great Revealer of the Father, conveying to us God's highest and kindest thought and exhibiting to us His nature and character. It is the same truth elsewhere expressed by John himself: "No man hath seen God at any time; the only begotten Son, which is in the bosom of the Father, he hath declared him" (1:18); and also in the later Epistles of the New Testament: "Who is the image of the invisible God" (Colossians 1:15); "Who being the brightness of [the Father's] glory, and the express image of his person" (Hebrews 1:3). What a beautiful conception it gives us of the mission of Jesus.

An ancient conqueror held in bondage the beautiful wife of his enemy. Again and again the unhappy prince had sent his petition for the return of her he loved better than his life. The conqueror sent no written reply, but one day, who should appear at the gates of the prince but the captive wife herself bearing this response: "The king has sent me to be myself the answer to your petitions." She was the personal word that satisfied all his desire as no language could.

So in answer to all man's questionings and cries, and all the heart's deep needs God speaks to us. God does not speak to us merely words of truth and promise, but sends the living answer, Jesus Himself, as the one great all-expressive Word which contains in it the substance of all other words and thoughts. He is to us not only the realization of God's purity, power and wisdom, but the expression of God's love.

## SECTION 2—THE CREATING WORD (John 1:3-4)

This also leads us back to the first chapter of Genesis and the record of creation. "God said, Let there be light: and there was light" (Genesis 1:3). This was the Personal Word, and by Him all things were made. This is amplified by the apostle Paul in Colossians 1:16, "For by him were all things created, that are in heaven, and that are in earth, visible and invisible, whether they be thrones, or dominions, or principalities, or powers: all things were created by him, and for him." And if the literal construction of these words is "in him were all things created," it would seem to teach that the material universe was really involved in Christ's own eternal being, and that He is its essential Head; and, perhaps, His own incarnation is in some sense connected with this thought.

The last link in the glorious chain, which unites the universe with the throne, is the person of Jesus combining in Himself both the Creator and the creation. Christ's relation to nature is a most practical truth. As the maker of our spirits and the framer of our bodies, He is the true supply of all the needs that He has created and the true restorer of our wrecked holiness and happiness. He is the true head of every human life, and apart from Him our being is abnormal and must be miserably lost. What an emphasis it gives to His humility to think that He who made all worlds and beings should lie as an infant on Mary's bosom.

## SECTION 3—CHRIST'S GLORY IN THE OLD TESTAMENT *(John 1:4-5, 9-10)*

These words refer to Christ's relation to the rational life and reason of man and God's manifested Presence in the Old Testament revelations, which He made successfully under the patriarchal and Mosaic dispensations. He was "the true Light, which lighteth every man" (John 1:9) in the sense of giving reason and intelligence to the human race. And "He was in the world" (1:10), not only in the rational nature which He gave to men, but especially in the manifestations of His will which He made to the Old Testament patriarchs and prophets. And yet, with a very few exceptions, "the world knew him not" (1:10). The very intelligence which He gave to the human mind was prostituted to intellectual pride and idolatrous worship.

The successive revelations made to Abraham, Moses and the prophets were all connected with the person of Christ, the great Angel of the Covenant, whom we can trace through all the stages of former dispensations. He is ever recognized in these revelations as the Son of God.

## SECTION 4—THE INCARNATE WORD  *(John 1:14)*

First we have the nature and fact of the incarnation in the literal translation of the Greek word, "He became flesh." This denotes true and actual humanity; not merely a body, but also a soul. There were not, however, two distinct persons. It was the same person who was the Eternal Word, who became a visible, tangible human being, possessing both natures but combining them in one person. It is not said he became *a man*, but He became *man*; in the widest sense "He is the Son of Man."

The exact meaning of this now becomes more vivid in the light of various heresies which have arisen in the church. Among these might be mentioned Apollinarianism, which teaches that the divine Word took on a human body, but not a human soul; Nestorianism, which teaches that He had two personalities, both a human and a divine; Eutichianism, which really makes Christ have a third nature through the incarnation; and Gnosticism, which represents His body as simply an illusion, and not really belonging to the Christ; and other less noted errors.

It is needless to speak concerning the process and method of the mystery of the Incarnation. It is enough for faith to know that the power of the Holy Ghost united the nature of God with the child of Mary in one divine and human personality which includes humanity in its widest sense and links Him with every race, sex and age as the real brother and head.

One of the latest errors respecting Christ is that of so-called Christian Science, which denies the existence of matter, and, therefore, the physical and material existence of Jesus Christ, regarding Him as merely a principle of rational mind. This is the heresy of which the apostle John has said, "He that believeth not that Jesus Christ is come in the flesh is not of God: and this is that spirit of antichrist, whereof ye have heard that it should come; and even now already is it in the world" (1 John 4:3, author's paraphrase).

Second, the human life of Christ on earth. He "dwelt among us" (John 1:14). Literally, this means, "He tabernacled among us." This describes His earthly life, which was as human as His birth and which constantly manifested, not only His humanity, but also His divine glory. There is an allusion here to the Hebrew tabernacle in the wilderness as a type of Jesus in His person and life.

Third, the manifested glory of the incarnate Christ. All through His earthly life it is witnessed by the apostles: "We beheld his glory, the glory as of the only begotten of the Father, full of grace and truth" (1:14). His whole life was a constant testimony of His divinity. The term glory, here applied to Christ's earthly life, is also an allusion to the glory of God manifested in the tabernacle and the temple (Exodus 16:10; 40:34; Ezekiel 1:28, etc.).

## THE ONLY BEGOTTEN

Another term is here introduced for the first time which we find frequently repeated afterwards in the New Testament: "The only begotten of the Father." This expression denotes the filial relation. The Son is in some ineffable sense the effulgence and offspring of the Father's life and yet of equal and co-eternal glory. The term also specifies this relationship as peculiar to Christ and absolutely without parallel. No other is a son of God in the sense in which He is, except, of course, His people, who through their union with Him are received into the fellowship of His very Sonship.

Two other expressions are used to characterize the manifested glory of His life, namely, *grace* and *truth*. These express the two great ideas that run through all the writings of John so constantly, namely, *love* and *light*. Grace is the expression of God's love, and truth denotes the light which He came to shed on the destinies of men. Thus the incarnate Word proves His own deity by the constant manifestation of His glory through His gracious words and works and His marvelous revelation of truth and light through His own teachings and example. The word, *truth,* literally means reality and expresses the idea that, in contrast with the mere types and shadows of the law, Christ is the actual fulfillment of the promises.

## SECTION 5—WITNESS OF JOHN (John 1:6, 8, 19, 30; 3:22-36)

Next, we have the witness of the great forerunner introduced. His advent is described in impressive language as one sent from God, and yet, in sharp distinction from the glorious person he came to identify, he is called "a man." He was especially called from the priestly line to represent the official witness of Judaism to the Son of God and to gather up the testimony of all the prophets. In his own last message, he came not to call attention to himself or his work, but for a witness of Christ, the true Light, and not merely that Israel might receive her Messiah, but with a wider scope, that "all men through him might believe" (John 1:7).

John's testimony involves:

a. The witness to the preexistence of Christ. "He was before me" (1:30). This necessarily implies His divinity for, humanly speaking, John was born before Jesus. Therefore, if Christ was before him, He must have had a prior and, therefore, divine existence.

b. Not only His preexistence, but His preeminence. "He is preferred before me, whose shoe's latchet I am not worthy to unloose" (1:27). John clearly recognizes Him as possessing the divinity and glory of the eternal God.

c. John recognizes Him as the Son of God (1:34).

d. John recognizes Him as the giver of the Holy Ghost: "the same is He which baptizeth with the Holy Ghost" (1:33). His relation to the other Person of the Trinity is as definite as to the Father. There could be no higher testimony to the glory of Jesus than to give Him His place of honor in connection with the ministry of the Holy Spirit, through whom the light of revelation had come and was still to come from God to man.

e. John testifies of Jesus, "the Lamb of God, which taketh away the sin of the world" (1:29), thus recognizing His sacrificial work and priestly character as the atoning Saviour for lost men. Then, respecting his own ministry, John describes himself as simply a voice, nothing in himself, but simply as a messenger declaring the words of another prior witness of the true object of man's hope and affections. How beautiful the picture of his humility, and how glorious the vision he brings of Jesus as the eternal Son of God, the Saviour of sinful men and the source of the Holy Ghost through whom we receive the light and life of His great redemption.

## SECTION 6—THE WITNESS OF THE HOLY GHOST (John 1:32)

This was the visible descent of the Holy Spirit upon Jesus, in the form of a dove, and was designed to be an open and manifest testimony to His Messiahship and divinity that no one could gainsay. It was also, as we learn from the other evangelists, accompanied by the voice of God, proclaiming, "This is my beloved Son, in whom I am well pleased" (Matthew 3:17).

To John himself this sign had already been promised as the special token of the Messiah. The voice of God had whispered to him, "Upon whom thou shalt see the Spirit descending, and remaining on him, the same is he which baptizeth with the Holy Ghost" (John 1:33). This is ever still the highest testimony that God can give to any of His servants. The same Holy Spirit is the witness of Christianity by His unceasing manifestations of grace and power in the ministry of God's servants and the lives of His children. The form in which the Holy Spirit came to Christ, as a dove, suggests the ideas of gentleness, peace and love as the special attributes of His life and ministry.

## SECTION 7—THE WITNESS OF THE FIRST DISCIPLES (John 1:37-49)

We have here the testimonies of Christ's earliest followers. Some of them had already been the disciples of John. At his testimony they left their former master and followed Jesus. Like all true disciples, they began to testify.

The first witness was Andrew, and his testimony was first given to his own brother, Simon. "We have found the Messias," was his glad message, "which is . . . the Christ" (1:41). Simon, in turn, comes also to the Saviour, and becomes henceforth His boldest witness. The next day Philip is called, at once follows the Master and immediately becomes himself a witness to his friend Nathaniel. "We have found," he says, "him of whom Moses in the law, and the prophets, did write, Jesus of Nazareth, the son of Joseph" (1:45).

Nathaniel's conservative spirit is disposed to question the ardor of his younger friend, but his doubts only serve to emphasize his own testimony when a little later he meets the Master himself. Under the searching glance of His omniscient eye, Nathaniel recognizes immediately His divine and Messianic character and exclaims, "Rabbi, thou art the Son of God; thou art the King of Israel" (1:49).

## SECTION 8—CHRIST'S WITNESS TO HIMSELF (John 1:50-51)

Jesus replies by appropriating to Himself the sublime symbol of

Jacob's ladder of which, perhaps, Nathaniel at the time had been reading. He represents Himself as the way of access between earth and heaven through whom henceforth the supernatural and stupendous manifestations of God are to be made known to His people. He adopts in His reply to Nathaniel a new title, "the Son of man." While it carries with it the sense of divine majesty and His superhuman dignity, it chiefly represents Him in His relations to humanity as the Brother, Redeemer and Head of the race with which He has forever become linked in His incarnation.

This may, therefore, be called His own witness to Himself. It fittingly closes the series of testimonies contained in this wonderful chapter: the Word, the Only Begotten of the Father, the Light, the Life of man, the Son of God, the Messiah, the King of Israel and now the Son of Man.

## SECTION 9—THE WITNESS OF HIS WORKS (John 2:1-11)

This miracle is recorded only by John, and the closing sentence connects it with the manifestation of His divine power and glory. "This beginning of miracles did Jesus in Cana of Galilee, and manifested forth his glory; and his disciples believed on him" (2:11). It was designed, therefore, as a special manifestation of His divine glory. Its deeper spiritual teachings we will afterward dwell more fully upon. Here it is enough to notice, it is God's first witness through the works of His beloved Son.

His mother seems to have expected some remarkable exhibition of His power, and yet He is most careful to guard Himself from being misunderstood even in His relations to her. His words, "Woman, what have I to do with thee?" (2:4) have placed an infinite gulf between the glory of the Son of God and even that blessed woman whom superstition has set up in a place of equal honor.

The force of the testimony is enhanced by the statement of its influence on His disciples. In consequence of this miracle they believed on Him, so that their testimony is really added to the miracle itself.

So far as this special miracle is concerned, we may notice first the power manifested in this instance over organic matter where there was no element of life to act spontaneously. It must therefore have been the direct result of Omnipotence. Secondly, the symbolical ideas suggested by the transformation of a lower into a higher substance, foreshadowing the character of His work as bringing the larger and richer blessings of the gospel to take the place of the old dispensation. Thirdly, the tender sympathy with human affections and joys which it suggested and the great fact that the ministry of Jesus was to be a ministry of love, and to raise His people to all gladness as suggested by the marriage feast.

## SECTION 10—HIS SECOND MIRACLE
## (John 2:13-17)

This instance has already been referred to at length in the other Gospels. It is well to link it with the chain of testimony to Christ's divine character of which it formed a part. It was the unanswerable token to the officials of Judaism of Christ's authority over the temple and the institutions of Moses. They did not attempt to resist or dispute the justice and righteousness of His stern judgment on their abuse of their sacred trust.

## SECTION 11—THE WITNESS OF HIS OWN DEATH
## AND RESURRECTION (John 2:18-22)

Having been asked by the Jews for a sign of His authority as a teacher and divine messenger, He gives them a hint in the language of a symbolism which faith might easily understand, and this token, "Destroy this temple, and in three days I will raise it up" (2:19). Their traditional ideas could only interpret His words in their literal sense; but His disciples afterward remembered that He had thus announced, in the very beginning, His death and resurrection as the supreme evidence of His being the true Messiah, the Son of God. This is still, and ever shall be, God's highest seal, to His beloved Son and the cornerstone of Christian evidence—declared to be the Son of God with power . . . by the resurrection from the dead (Romans 1:4).

## SECTION 12—WITNESS OF THE COMMON
## PEOPLE (John 2:23-25)

The miracles already referred to were followed at this time by many similar exhibitions of His power. The result was that large numbers of the people had accepted Him as the Messiah. But that conviction which comes from the evidence of signs can never be fully depended upon, so we read that Jesus did not value greatly the adherence of even this multitude. He did not commit Himself to them, because He knew what was in man; still, their testimony to Him had its place and value. How unsuitable to them must have been the evidences of His authority and claims. There is undoubtedly an allusion here in the very meaning of the words employed, to the superficial character of the faith of the people. It was rather the result of wonder at His astonishing power than of a personal confidence in, and devotion to Him.

## SECTION 13—THE WITNESS OF THE RULERS (John 3:1-13)

Here we find a leading Rabbi coming to Him, timidly but honestly, and expressing without reserve the confidence of the class he represented in the new Master that had come among them. "We know that thou art a teacher come from God: for no man can do these miracles that thou doest, except God be with him" (3:2). This is a very strong testimony, and yet the Lord Himself saw in it its essential defect. It wholly lacked a deep spiritual knowledge of Christ and His teachings and the most essential principles of the kingdom of heaven. Therefore, Christ at once ignores the confidence of Nicodemus and presses him in order to unfold the true meaning of His work and mission to the wondering Pharisee.

We are not told of the immediate result, but we know that a few months later this man was not ashamed to stand up in the very midst of the highest council of the nation and claim for Christ a fair hearing and, still later, to go to the very governor himself with Joseph and claim His body for honorable burial. The witness of Nicodemus grew at length to be one of the grandest testimonies which the Lord ever received.

## SECTION 14—JOHN'S SECOND TESTIMONY TO CHRIST (John 3:25-36)

Christ had now become fully established as a teacher, and

some of John's disciples, jealous of their master's honor, came to him to report and complain about the success of his rival. The spirit of the Baptist shines out again, in still more beautiful and heavenly light, as he modestly takes his true place at the feet of the greater Master and bears a still higher testimony to His pre-eminence.

He reminds them that no man is anything in himself, and can receive nothing except what is given him from heaven. His position, he again reminds them, is not one of any personal consequence or importance, but simply that of a witness to another in whose glory he is glad to be lost sight of. He is but the friend of the bridegroom and does not come to absorb the attention of the bride, or even the spectators, but simply to wait upon the bridegroom and rejoice in the greater love and honor which He receives.

It is necessary, therefore, that the more successful his ministry becomes, the more prominent his Master will be and the more will he pass out of sight. The very conditions of his ministry are such that "He must increase, but I must decrease" (3:30). Like the morning star, he is the herald of the dawn, and the rising sun buries his light in a brighter effulgence. He then proceeds to give a most distinct and excellent witness to the person and glory of Jesus.

a. He declares that He cometh from above and afterwards explains this to be from heaven.

b. He says that He is above all, referring not only to His pre-eminence above all beings, but His sovereign authority over all things.

c. He declares that the things which He testifieth are not through the witness of another, but are the results of his own direct knowledge—"what he hath seen and heard, that he testifieth" (3:32).

d. He declares that all who receive His testimony thus bear witness that it is true. This must mean, therefore, that His testimony is God's testimony and that He is God.

The figurative expression, "Has set to his seal" (3:33), expresses very strongly the faith with which we should receive the testimony of Christ; not only assenting to it with our mind, but committing our entire being to it by the most solemn acts and sanctions of faith.

e. Next, he declares that God hath sent Christ in a special sense not true of any other messenger. "He whom God hath sent" (3:34). Of John it was said that he "was a man sent from God" (1:6), but the meaning here is stronger. This Messenger was sent by God, in a most direct sense, to represent Himself. The words which He speaks are the very words of God.

f. He possesses the Holy Spirit without measure. This is not true, or possible, of any finite being, and therefore it is an attestation of Christ's divinity. "God giveth not the Spirit by measure unto him" (3:34). All the fullness of the Godhead dwells in Him (Colossians 2:9); all, including both the nature of the Father and the infinite resources of the Holy Ghost.

g. John further declares that Christ is the special object of the Father's love and that He "hath given all things into his hand" (John 3:35). To Him has been committed the government, the fullness of the divine attributes and the administration of the whole plan of redemption—even the judgment of all men in the Last Day. This is parallel to the expression in Hebrews 1:1-2: "God, who at sundry times and in divers manners spake in times past unto the fathers by the prophets, Hath in these last days spoken unto us by his Son, whom he hath appointed heir of all things."

h. In consequence of this high commission and investiture of authority and power, He has therefore become the only Saviour of sinful men. Their destiny depends upon their reception or rejection of Him: "He that believeth on the Son hath everlasting life: and he that believeth not the Son shall not see life; but the wrath of God abideth on him" (3:36).

## SECTION 15—WITNESS OF THE SAMARITANS (John 4:28-30, 40-42)

The testimony of these people is the more remarkable because of their traditional prejudice and jealousy with respect to everything Jewish. It is the more emphatic because it was perfectly spontaneous and called forth by no great miracle on the part of Christ or testimony to Him from others. It was wholly elicited by the moral and spiritual influence of His presence and character and His simple conversation with the Samaritan woman and her countrymen. This represents the instinctive testimony of the human heart, and even of the sinful heart, to the Saviour and to the gospel when brought into living contact.

There is perhaps no more remarkable or beautiful evidence of the divinity of Jesus than the consciousness He impressed upon this poor woman, as He quietly talked with her, that He was the searcher and creator of her heart as well as its Saviour. "Come, see a man, which told me all things that ever I did: is not this the Christ?" (4:29). The same impression was produced upon the hearts of the rest of the Samaritans: "Now we believe," they said, "not because of thy saying: for we have heard him ourselves, and know that this is indeed the Christ, the Saviour of the world" (4:42).

Something like this is often the result of the first contact of the Gospel with heathen hearts. The same conviction always comes to the converted soul in the moment of its first coming to the real Saviour. It knows by evidence, which nothing could shake and nothing could add to, that He is indeed the Christ—and the divine Christ. Therefore, to every soul that knows the Saviour personally, this is the supreme evidence of Christianity—its own personal experience and acquaintance with Jesus.

## SECTION 16—CHRIST'S SECOND GALILEAN MIRACLE (John 4:46-54)

There are some things peculiar about this miracle. In His conversation with the nobleman, the Master implies that there is a danger even that the signs and miracles by which He has already attested His character and commission will prove a snare to those of feeble faith—that the evidence of the people will be so based upon these, that they will not be able to believe without constant signs. Therefore, in this case, He refuses to go down to Capernaum to heal the dying boy but requires the father to believe without any evidence, except the naked word of Jesus, that his son is really healed by that simple word.

The father's faith proves equal to the great demand, and he immediately departs, to find, to his unutterable joy, his child restored and his servants on their way to meet him with the glad tidings. The faith of this man was a higher testimony, therefore, to Christ than the evidence which had hitherto been based upon His visible miracles. The fact also that this healing was produced without His personal presence, and simply by His naked word as it traversed the intervening space and commanded the forces of nature and disease to obey His almighty will, enhanced its weight.

## SECTION 17—CHRIST'S APPEAL TO THE TESTIMONY OF HIS WORKS (John 5:17-31)

This testimony immediately followed one of the mightiest of His miracles, namely, the healing of the impotent man at the pool of Bethesda in Jerusalem. It had been followed by a bitter persecution on the part of the Jewish rulers, especially on account of Christ's ignoring the claims of the Sabbath by healing this man on that day. The Lord vindicates His work by the lofty claim that His works are coordinate with His Father's and of equal authority. The Father works on the Sabbath day by sustaining the material creation, and Christ claims the equal right to work in the spiritual world for the relief of His people.

This was Christ's own highest testimony hitherto to Himself, and they readily understood it to mean the claim of an absolute equality with God. This Jesus fully acknowledges in the discourse which follows in which He states that His works are in absolute and uninterrupted unity with the Father and are of equal power and glory, including even the resurrection of the dead, the future judgment and the quickening of the spiritually dead in the present time. In consequence of this He dares to claim, what they consider blasphemy, "That all men should honor the Son, even as they honor the Father" (5:23). Later in the 36th verse, Christ again applies to the witness of His works. "The same works that I do, bear witness of me, that the Father hath sent me."

## SECTION 18—CHRIST'S APPEAL TO THE WITNESS OF JOHN (John 5:32-35)

They had already received John as a divine messenger. Now the Lord appeals to their consistency, and the necessity of receiving John's witness concerning Himself, if they were consistent. At the same time He bears a very high testimony Himself to John as "a burning and a shining light" (5:35). "I know that the witness which He witnesseth of me is true" (5:32), He says. At the same time, He does not need the witness of John but appeals directly to His Father's testimony and the evidence of His works. He only refers to John as a witness for their sakes, and because they readily received him as one of their own prophets. "I receive not testimony from man: but these things I say, that ye might be saved" (5:34).

## SECTION 19—CHRIST'S APPEAL TO HIS FATHER'S WITNESS  (John 5:36-38)

In these words Christ appeals to the testimony which the Father had given at His baptism with His own living voice, thus implying that the fact that they did not receive Him is the strongest evidence that they are not even the people of God—that they do not know the Father's voice or believe His word.

## SECTION 20—CHRIST'S APPEAL TO THE SCRIPTURES  (John 5:39-47)

Their very own Scriptures, He tells them, contain the clearest intimation of His coming and character. "Moses wrote of Me, and if ye had believed Moses, ye would have believed Me. Ye search the Scriptures, in which ye think ye have eternal life, and they are they which testify of Me" (5:46, 39, author's paraphrase).

The Mosaic system was a beautiful and instructive type and prophecy of Jesus. We cannot understand even the institutions and teachings of Moses apart from the gospel. They had wholly misunderstood their own Scriptures, and thus rejecting Christ, even Moses would be a witness against them. Thus we triumphantly sum up the entire series of testimonies by which God has attested His divine character and Messianic claims. Over all might be appropriately recorded the verse already quoted, "These are written, that ye might believe that Jesus is the Christ, the Son of God; and that believing ye might have life through his name" (20:31).

## SECTION 21—TESTIMONY OF THE MULTITUDE (John 6:11-15)

This is the testimony of the multitude who had been fed miraculously by the multiplied bread and fishes. It is one of Christ's most impressive miracles, showing His absolute command over all the laws and forces of nature. The scale upon which it was wrought was so magnificent that it left the profoundest impression on the multitudes who witnessed it. So much so, indeed, that in the enthusiasm of the moment they impetuously determined to compel Him to become the leader of a great popular movement and to allow them to make Him their actual king. Of course, this was but a superficial and even a selfish movement. He knew their hearts better than they themselves did, and a few days afterwards declared to them, "Ye seek me, not because ye saw the miracles, but because ye did eat of the loaves and were filled" (6:26).

The Greek word in this last sentence denotes the grossest, the most animal satisfaction. They wanted a king that could gratify their earthly desires and give them immunity from laboring and suffering. They had no appreciation of Christ's higher character and teaching. At the same time, their testimony, on this occasion, was sincere and spontaneous—as far as they knew themselves—and bears witness to the power of Christ and the influence of His mighty works.

## SECTION 22—THE TESTIMONY OF NATURE (John 6:18-21)

This sublime miracle is also recorded by the other evangelists, but here it is added as an emphatic testimony to the omnipotent power of Christ that the moment He entered the ship, immediately it was at the land whither they went. Matthew and Mark tell us that the wind also ceased.

The elements of nature recognized their Master's touch. They not only gave Him a pathway upon the stormy waves, but also hushed their voices in instant subserviency to His will. Even space and distance were annihilated at His coming, and the little vessel dropped into her haven without a rippling wave or disturbing element.

These were both signs as well as miracles and designed to pre-pare the hearts of His disciples to understand that power that can work independently of all human means and agencies. That power can either use or ignore second causes and material things in the fulfillment of His will.

## SECTION 23—THE TESTIMONY OF PETER (John 6:66-69)

The feeding of the five thousand had been followed by the remarkable discussion of the following Sabbath in the syna-gogue of Capernaum. In this address He had attempted to un-fold the deeper meaning of the miracles and to reveal Himself as the true source and sustenance of His people's life, both for soul and body, under the figure of the Living Bread. These pro-found and beautiful teachings were met by captious question-ings and cavilings on the part of the Pharisees. At the close of His address the greater portion of His Galilean followers be-came offended and disgusted. Many of His disciples, we are told, went back and walked no more with Him. For a moment the Master seems to have almost doubted the chosen twelve; at least, He gave them the opportunity of making their own choice. Turning to them He asks, "Will ye also go away?" (6:67). The question is immediately answered by the impetuous Peter in a noble testimony and confession of Christ, which shows that although they dimly understood as yet the full meaning of His teachings, yet they felt in their deepest hearts that these teachings were the true satisfaction and life of their own hearts—that He was indeed the Christ, the Son of the liv-ing God.

This beautiful testimony comprehends both parts of the combined witness which John's Gospel was intended to unfold, namely, that Jesus is the Christ, the Son of God, and life through His name. Peter recognizes Him as the Christ, the Son of the living God, and also the Author of life eternal. The words of his confession are exceedingly positive and emphatic. It is not a mere opinion, but "We believe, and are sure" (6:69), he says. Literally, the original means, "We have believed, and have come to know."

It was more than even believing. It had risen to a spiritual consciousness of and acquaintance with Himself which had rendered doubt henceforth impossible. Thus his identification of Christ as the Messiah is equally explicit—that Christ is the Christ of prophecy and of Jewish expectation.

The true reading of the next clause seems to be, "the Holy One of God." This is the form found in the earliest and best manuscripts. This would indicate even more strongly the apostle's conception of His higher nature as one who had come to earth unstained by human sin and possessing the essential nature of the infinitely holy God.

## SECTION 24—THE WITNESS OF EVERY HUMAN CONSCIENCE *(John 7:14-17)*

Jesus here announces the true touchstone by which His teachings and all others may be tested. The proof is in the practice. "He that will honestly do, shall certainly know" (7:17, author's paraphrase). The best way to be convinced of the truth of Christianity is to test it. Any man who will take the simple and holy teachings of Jesus and honestly practice them according to the light that God gives, shall have an answering witness in his own experience which will leave no doubt of their truth.

In trying this test, we must, of course, follow the Master's own directions and begin at the beginning with a life of sincere dependence and simple trust, and then follow it by implicit and loving obedience. He who does this will always find the result in his own inward peace and happiness and the fruits of lasting blessing in his life and influence. Many of the most remarkable examples of Christian faith and usefulness in the church today have been saved from utter atheism by simply following this direction. This, after all, is the strongest evidence of Christianity.

## SECTION 25—TESTIMONY OF THE COMMON PEOPLE AT JERUSALEM *(John 7:25-40)*

The events described in this chapter transpired at Jerusalem during the Feast of Tabernacles. Day after day the Saviour had abundantly taught in the very midst of His enemies until the multitudes were amazed at His fearless boldness and the Pharisees were paralyzed and afraid to arrest or hinder Him. His wonderful teachings reached the very depths of many hearts and set all deeply questioning.

Some asked, "How knoweth this man letters, having never learned?" (7:15). "When Christ cometh, will he do more miracles than these which man hath done?" (7:31). Some said, "He is a good man: others said, Nay; but he deceiveth the people" (7:12). Even the doubters were impressed with His courage and said, "Is not this he, whom they seek to kill? But, lo, he speaketh boldly, and they say nothing unto him. Do the rulers know indeed that this is the very Christ?" (7:25-26).

Many at length dared to say, "Of a truth this is the Prophet" (7:40). The Pharisees saw that their hold upon the people was waning and that His audacious courage and wonderful teachings were winning the hearts of the multitude. Something needed to be done instantly, at least to show a consistent front on their part.

## SECTION 26—THE OFFICERS SENT TO ARREST HIM (John 7:32, 44-46)

Alarmed at the influence which Christ was gaining and the effects of their own inaction, the Pharisees at length ventured to attempt Christ's arrest. They sent a body of officers with authority for that purpose. It was while they were lying in wait for Him that Christ delivered the sublime message in the last days of the feast, recorded in John 7:37-38.

We can imagine something of the effect of this lofty eloquence and its striking fitness to the occasion. Doubtless there was much added which was not recorded and filled by the situation with a thousand details of tender and impressive meaning. At least, the effect upon the officers was like that of some magic spell. As they listened, they forgot all about their purpose in coming. When they awoke from the spell of His eloquence and found themselves in the presence of the Master, the only excuse they could give for their failure was the admiring testimony, "Never man spake like this man" (7:46).

## SECTION 27—CHRIST'S OWN TESTIMONY TO HIMSELF *(John 8:13-30)*

For the second time the Lord now bears witness to Himself and applies to His Father's witness as confirming it. These two witnesses, He claims, are sufficient, even according to their own law, to establish His authority. Their inability to understand this testimony was no evidence of its failure but was simply the result of their own ignorance of the Father as well as the Son.

All through this chapter the Lord lays bare their absolute blindness of heart, even to the meaning of their own institutions. "If God were your Father," He says, "ye would love Me: because I came forth from God" (8:42, author's paraphrase). "He that is of God heareth God's words: ye therefore hear them not, because ye are not of God" (8:47).

Even Abraham, whom they called their father, beheld in the distance His coming day and rejoiced in the prospect of it; but they, who called themselves the children of Abraham and the children of God, are even trying to kill the very One whom Abraham worshiped and whom God recognized as His dear Son. Their true father, therefore, is neither God nor Abraham, but the devil, who has been a liar and murderer from the beginning and who is now prompting them in their unbelief and murderous hate toward Him.

## SECTION 28—TESTIMONY OF THE BLIND MAN *(John 9:8-33)*

This miracle was intended to illustrate the special teaching of Jesus at the Feast of Tabernacles that He was the Light of the world. As such, He gives sight to this poor sufferer and afterwards opens his inner vision to know the truth and to behold His own divine glory. The miracle of his healing was enough to convince the blind man that Jesus was the Son of God, but to the Pharisees it only became another occasion for captiousness and questioning.

With his simple common sense the blind man was enabled to comprehend the doubts of Christ's enemies. He treated them with undisguised impatience and contempt. When they came to question him, he frankly told them the wonderful story of his healing and added, with a decisive confidence, "One thing I know, that, whereas I was blind, now I see" (9:25).

As they question him still more, he sarcastically asks, "I have told you already, and ye did not hear: wherefore would ye hear it again? will ye also be his disciples?" (9:27). And then as they heap abuse on him and his Master, he gives way to his utter astonishment at these would-be teachers: "Why herein is a marvelous thing, that ye know not from whence he is, and yet he hath opened mine eyes. Now we know that God heareth not sinners: but if any man be a worshipper of God, and doeth his will, him he heareth. . . . If this man were not of God, he could do nothing" (9:30-31, 33).

The second occasion of his plain speaking led to his expulsion from the synagogue with harshness and cruelty. The Lord Jesus, however, finds him, and now gives him a still deeper revelation of Himself as the Son of God. With the same simple frankness with which he believed before, he now accepts the higher truth. Falling at His feet in reverential worship, he becomes, in a deeper and higher sense, a disciple of the Lord Jesus whom he has so nobly confessed.

## SECTION 29—CHRIST'S THIRD TESTIMONY TO HIMSELF *(John 10:22-33)*

This is Christ's most emphatic and explicit witness. His language is intended to be unequivocal and to claim absolute equality with God. This is rendered indisputable by the interpretation which they put upon His words and which He did not contradict. They evidently believed Him to mean equality with the Father. Denouncing it as blasphemy, they attempted to stone Him for His profanity.

Had they been wrong in this idea, honesty would have compelled Him to contradict or correct them. On the contrary, He repeats more strongly His previous claims and calls upon His Father's witness, through His works, to the truth of His assumption. "If I do not the works of my Father," He says, "believe me not. But if I do, though ye believe not me, believe the works: that ye may know, and believe, that the Father is in me, and I in him" (10:37-38).

## SECTION 30—TESTIMONY OF THE RESURRECTION OF LAZARUS *(John 11:41-45)*

This stupendous miracle was God's most signal testimony to His Son, excepting only Christ's own resurrection. It was not only a triumph over death but over the corruption of the grave. It was as stupendous in power as the creation of the human race, and it left no doubt of the divinity of the Christ on every unprejudiced mind. Of course, His enemies were perverted by prejudice and determined to resist the effect of such evidence. They acknowledged, "This man doeth many miracles. If we let him thus alone, all men will believe on him" (11:47-48).

## SECTION 31—TESTIMONY OF CAIAPHAS *(John 11:47-52)*

This was a very remarkable witness by a high priest of the Jewish order uttered in the ecclesiastical council, the Sanhedrin. We are told that it was inspired by the Holy Ghost and not his own thought or wisdom. He declared that it was expedient "that one man should die for the people . . . And not for that nation only, but that also he should gather together in one the children of God that were scattered abroad" (11:50, 52).

This extraordinary testimony, summing up, as it did, the whole spirit of prophecy and the essential facts of redemption, is one of the sublime examples of the way in which God can use even wicked men as His instruments. Henceforth it gave a spirit of religious inspiration to the wicked and malicious Pharisees, under cover of which they henceforth prosecuted with double diligence their murderous intent.

## SECTION 32—TESTIMONY OF MARY *(John 12:3-8)*

This was the witness of a loving heart to its Lord. It was not only the witness of love, but also of the most farsighted and illuminated faith. She saw in Him not only her Lord, but also her dying Saviour. Anointing His body for burial before the cross and the tomb, she was perhaps the only one of His disciples who really understood the meaning of His life and death. It was therefore accepted by Him with peculiar delight, and the odor of the ointment has filled heaven and earth ever since.

## SECTION 33—WITNESS OF THE NATION TO JESUS (John 12:12-19)

This popular outburst of patriotic enthusiasm, in which the whole nation for a time united, was intended as a divine witness to His Messiahship and as a type of the time when He shall be welcomed to the throne of Israel by the race that crucified and rejected Him. The psalms they sung, the ascriptions they uttered, were all connected with the highest hopes of Judaism and the most sacred and divine worship. No wonder that the Pharisees were filled with consternation and exclaimed, "Perceive ye how ye prevail nothing? behold, the world is gone after him" (12:19).

## SECTION 34—THE WITNESS OF THE GENTILES (John 12:20-22)

The coming of these Greeks to Jesus represented the reaching out of the heart of the Gentile nations towards God and the deep hunger in every human heart crying out inarticulately for that which only Christ can satisfy. The deep need of humanity is here expressed, "We would see Jesus" (12:21). Not always do they know their own need, but when he is truly lifted up before them, all true hearts recognize and receive Him.

To Him, on the eve of His rejection, this incident was a prophecy of the time when He will draw all men unto Him. Even already we have seen this gloriously anticipated from time to time in the history of missions, in the strange turning of the heathen heart to the gospel and the crucified Saviour when simply and truthfully presented. The savages of Greenland resisted for years all the moral teachings of the Moravian missionaries, but when they began to tell the story of Jesus and read the third chapter of John, their hearts were completely broken down. The Gospel became its own witness to their deeper consciousness.

There is something in Jesus that finds a response in the hearts when the barriers of ignorance and prejudice are removed; but there is no sublimer witness to the truth of Christianity than its adaptation to the conscious needs of our lost humanity.

## SECTION 35—THE VOICE FROM HEAVEN (John 12:27-33)

This was the third direct witness of the Father's voice to His Son. The first had been given at His baptism, the second on the Mount of Transfiguration. This was distinctly audible to the people, although perhaps none of them understood it explicitly. To some it seemed like a peal of thunder: to others an angel's voice. Jesus declared that it was designed as the Father's special testimony for their sakes.

It is remarkable that this glorious testimony to Jesus followed immediately His own profoundest declaration with reference to His humiliation and sufferings. He had fully recognized and expressed His great mission of suffering death as the essential condition of His ultimate glory. The corn of wheat must die before it can bring forth fruit, and He must reach His throne by way of the cross; nor He alone, but all His followers too.

For a moment He shrinks back from the awful vision and cries out in His shrinking human consciousness, "Father, save Me from this hour" (12:27). But instantly He rises into victory and adds, "Father, glorify thy name" (12:28), thus accepting the cross and all its shame and consecrating Himself to the great sacrifice.

"Father, glorify thy name!" Then it is that the testimony of heaven seals His consecration and witnesses to His acceptance. The voice of God proclaims, "I have both glorified it, and will glorify it again" (12:28). Jesus accepts the testimony, and rises to meet it in the lofty assurance of faith and victory. "Now," He cries, "is the judgment of this world: now shall the prince of this world be cast out. And I, if I be lifted up from the earth, will draw all men unto me" (12:31-32).

A little later in this chapter Jesus refers again to His Father's witness (12:47-50) and solemnly reminds His hearers that rejection of His message is also the rejection of His Father and shall be the witness against them in the Last Day.

## SECTION 36—THE WITNESS OF ISAIAH (John 12:37-41)

The Lord quotes this verse to explain the unbelief of so many of the people, showing them it was simply what Isaiah, the ancient prophet, had foretold and referring especially to two chapters in which that most illustrious of Judah's prophets had borne witness of His sufferings and glory.

The first quotation (12:38) is from the fifty-third chapter of Isaiah—the vision of the Messiah's sufferings and humiliation. The other reference, in verses 40 and 41, is to the sixth chapter of Isaiah and the sublime vision of the heavenly glory contained therein, which the evangelist tells us had special reference to Jesus Himself and which is manifestly a vision of Jehovah in the midst of all the majesty of His heavenly throne. To ascribe such glory to a mortal would indeed be the height of profanity.

## SECTION 37—CHRIST'S OWN CONSCIOUSNESS (John 13:3)

There is a profound, subtle force in this verse. The very humiliation of Jesus, and His own voluntariness in it, while, to the outward sense, might seem to be a contradiction of His preeminence, is the most perfect proof of His real dignity. It was because He knew that the Father had given all things into His hands, that He was come from God and went to God, that He could so easily sacrifice and abase Himself. True dignity can afford to stoop. False pride, with no intrinsic loftiness, is always trying to lift itself up. One who knows he has an illustrious name is not always trying to proclaim it.

Jesus knew that He was divine and could not be misunderstood, therefore He was willing to stoop to the lowest place and set a perfect example of sacrifice and service. Never did He seem so divine to His disciples, as when He knelt at their feet in the garb of a servant to wash away their stains.

When does He for a moment lose the consciousness of His dignity in all this menial service? "Ye call me Master and Lord," He adds, as He sits down again, "and ye say well, for so I am. If I then, your Lord and Master, have washed your feet; ye ought also to wash one another's feet" (13:13-14). And so, like Him, the more fully we realize our divine calling, the more willingly will we take the humblest place; and the less we know of the glory of our sonship, the more will we contend for the honors of earth and preeminence among our brethren.

## SECTION 38—CHRIST'S TESTIMONY TO HIS COMING GLORIFICATION *(John 13:31-32)*

This announcement immediately followed the withdrawal of Judas from the company of the disciples and the presence of the Lord. His retirement lifted a great load from the mind of Jesus, and His spirit rose at once to this joyful utterance. Freely accepting all the consequences of Judas' betrayal and the cross and all its shame, He declares, "Now is the Son of man glorified" (13:31).

His death was to be His glorification as the Son of Man. It was also to bring unutterable glory to God, and it was to be followed by the glorification of Christ Himself—not merely as the Son of Man, but also in His own divine being and nature. Over all the dark and overshadowed valley of the garden and the cross He sees, immediately beyond, the glory of His Father and His own eternal exaltation. "For the joy that was set before him [He] endured the cross, despising the shame, and is [now] set down at the right hand of the throne of God" (Hebrews 12:2).

## SECTION 39—CHRIST'S DISCOURSE AT THE PASSOVER TABLE *(John 14:1-11)*

Perhaps there is no higher testimony to the divinity of Christ than the sublime consciousness expressed in these words. For a mortal to utter such language would be offensive and unspeakably profane. No man has ever dared to use such language. The very utterance of it would carry with it its own answer in the manifest consciousness of its extravagance. But in the case of Christ there is no such feeling as we hear Him say, "Ye believe in God, believe also in me" (John 14:1). "I am in the Father, and the Father in me" (14:10). "If ye had known me, ye should have known my Father also: and from henceforth ye know him, and have seen him" (14:7). "If ye shall ask anything in my name, I will do it" (14:14).

All this is so calm, so free from any idea of assumption or of having uttered anything extraordinary; such an obvious simplicity and sense of truthfulness and reality pervade it that it bears the irresistible consciousness to every unprejudiced heart of the genuineness of His claims and the loftiness of His character. Even in human character we can always detect the borrowed feathers of pretentiousness and recognize the natural nobility that sits so easily on lofty spirits and kingly natures. So the portrait of Jesus given in His own words is its own safe witness. The sustained character which He maintains all through this marvelous address is simply superhuman and beyond the power of man's invention.

Not only do we trace in every sentence this divine consciousness of His relation to His Father, but the way in which He reveals Himself as the life and strength of His people, bestowing upon them with kingly bounty His grace, His intercession, His peace, His supernatural power, His spiritual presence in their hearts and the living reality of all this, as it has been experienced and seen in the hearts and lives of millions for more than fifty generations, is, to every Christian heart, the deepest, most satisfying testimony to the reality and divinity of Jesus.

## SECTION 40—THE WITNESS OF THE HOLY SPIRIT (John 14:16-20, 26; 16:7-14)

The Holy Spirit had already borne witness to the Lord Jesus at His baptism, but here He is introduced as His divine Successor in the consummation of His mediatorial work and the perpetual witness through the coming ages to His person, His truth and His glory. He is to be the interpreter of all that Christ has said and to make real to the faith and consciousness of His people, through divine and inward illumination, that which would otherwise be but an intellectual apprehension. He was to bring the vision as well as the light. He was to bring to their remembrance all things that Christ had already said, and then to lead them into further truths which they were not now able to bear; even opening the vista of the future and showing them things to come.

Above all He was to be the special witness of Christ, and testify not of them, nor even of Himself, but personally of Jesus. And even to the world, which could not yet receive Him, He was to bring persuasions as no human arguments or persuasions could come, leading them to see their sin, their Saviour and the necessity of their separation from the world and the powers of evil.

## SECTION 41—HIS INTERCESSORY PRAYER (John 17:5, 8, 23-24)

There is no place nor time where the soul is so unfolded spiritually as the hour of solitary prayer, especially in some great crisis of need or suffering. This chapter is the opening of the curtains of the inner sanctuary of Christ's heart and the unsealing of the very Holy of Holies itself. Here, above all other places, we may expect the truest and deepest expression of His consciousness, and it is still the same as in His parting words to His disciples.

Calmly and sublimely He still takes His exalted and supreme place in His Father's fellowship, speaks of the glory which He had before the world was, assumes His perfect unity with Him as the very pattern of the oneness of His disciples and claims the sanctification, preservation and glorification of His people by kingly right, with the majestic and imperative words which none but the equal of God could utter, "Father, I will." Surely no one can look upon this scene without the deepest conviction of His conscious Deity and the feeling that to assume such claims and rights, and constantly sustain the lofty character to the close, would have been as impossible for a mere man as it would have been profane.

## SECTION 42—HIS VOLUNTARY SUBMISSION TO HIS ENEMIES (John 18:4-8)

This remarkable instance, recorded only by John, bears the strongest testimony to the divine character of Jesus and the perfect voluntariness of His death. The men who came to arrest Him had no power to hurt Him or touch Him without His free consent. A silent look into their faces was enough to paralyze their strength and prostrate them on the ground at His feet. It was only when He willingly yielded Himself to their hands, that they were able to bind Him. Throughout His entire sufferings it was every moment true that man could have no power over Him except it was given from above. He could truly say, "I lay down my life for the sheep. No man taketh it from me, but I lay it down of myself. I have power to lay it down, and I have power to take it again" (10:15,18).

## SECTION 43—TESTIMONY OF HIS BAFFLED ACCUSERS (John 18:19-24, 29-30)

In all this record of His trial there was not a single specific charge laid against Him by the Jews. Even when they sent Him to Pilate, they simply assumed that the governor would take their word for it and condemn Him without trial. Their general charge that "He is a malefactor," and their inability to formulate a single indictment that could stand against the test of Roman law, is the highest testimony of His innocence and blamelessness.

Looking in their faces He could appeal to those who heard Him, and say, "If I have spoken evil, bear witness of the evil" (18:23). They had no answer but violence and vagueness. Indeed they never had any charge to bring against Him but simply that which was His supremest glory, namely, His claim that He was the Son of God. It was really for this that He was crucified at last.

## SECTION 44—TESTIMONY OF PILATE (John 18:38; 19:4, 12, 19)

The Roman governor, finding that they had no charge against Him, refused to take their vague and general demand for His condemnation. He asked explicitly what accusation they brought. Getting no satisfactory reply, he questioned Him personally himself. The result was a deep conviction of Christ's innocence which ever afterwards filled his soul. At last it became a terrible fear and led him into that strange conflict between his own conscience and the mean and selfish desire to please the people which terminated at length in the Saviour's crucifixion. But up to the close, Pilate's repeated testimony was borne to the Saviour's innocence. The inscription which he had placed upon His cross and refused to change was the highest testimony to this conviction. He did not say this is Jesus of Nazareth, a criminal, or a pretended king, but literally and unequivocally, "This is Jesus of Nazareth, the King of the Jews."

## SECTION 45—TESTIMONY FROM THE CROSS
### (John 19:23, 28, 36-38)

These several passages combine the witness of the prophetical Scriptures to the sufferings of Christ, showing how literally and wonderfully every particular of the ancient picture was fulfilled, thus identifying Him as the true Messiah of Hebrew promise and hope. John's purpose in recording these minute details is to establish the point which his Gospel was designed to prove, namely, that Jesus is the Christ. And so we find him, more frequently than any other evangelist, saying, "that the Scripture might be fulfilled."

The very parting of His garments, the consuming thirst that parched His tongue, the premature death that exempted Him from the breaking of His limbs and even the interment of His body in the tomb of the wealthy Joseph, were all fulfillments of scriptural predictions and marks of unmistakable identity.

## SECTION 46—TESTIMONY OF HIS
## RESURRECTION (John 20:11)

This, of course, is the supreme evidence of the divinity and Messiahship of Christ. The details which were given by John have, however, a special force. First, there is the evident unexpectedness of it by these simple disciples. None of them seem to have had the faintest dream of His literal resurrection. Peter and John were both astonished, and Mary Magdalene was so unprepared for it that she did not at first recognize the Lord until He called her very name. This gives enhanced weight to the conclusion which was forced upon them by His actual appearance again.

Next we have the explicit details which the narrative gives of the persons and places and the most trifling circumstances connected with His resurrection: the open door, the linen clothes and the napkin that was about His head wrapped together in a place by itself. All these points have a very positive weight in the question of evidence, which every judicial mind will fully appreciate.

Then we have the explicit testimony of John, that "he saw, and believed" (20:8). It was not an afterthought, but the instant and instinctive conviction of his whole mind that the Lord was really risen from the dead. But most conclusive of all is the testimony of Mary, all the stronger because of her perplexity at first and her womanly disappointment at not finding the body, then her delighted and enraptured surprise when she recognized the Lord Himself. Throwing herself at His feet, she poured out the fullness of her confidence and joy in the one cry, "Rabboni."

All this evidence is confirmed by the subsequent appearance of Christ to His disciples, as narrated in this and the following chapter

## SECTION 47—TESTIMONY OF THOMAS (John 20:24-28)

This is perhaps the strongest witness of all from the fact that it has for its background the strongest unbelief, for Thomas had fully determined that he would not be deceived. His very love to the Master had made him afraid of any false hope. He did not expect His resurrection, and he could not bear to have an impostor palmed upon his loving heart. He therefore demanded the most tangible and unmistakable demonstration and received it—even more than he asked. Indeed, after the answer came, he was not only satisfied but ashamed that he had asked such tokens. He threw himself at the feet of his blessed Master with one inexpressible cry of unquestioning confidence and everlasting consecration, "My Lord and my God" (20:28).

The conviction of Thomas ought to be a sufficient answer to every honest doubter. It is to be observed, however, that the evidence which convinced Thomas the most forcibly was not the mere external appearance of Christ, or the physical marks of identity which he expected, but that divine omniscience which had already searched the heart of Thomas and made him feel that he was in the presence, not only of the Nazarene, but the all-see-ing God. And so, still, the strongest evidence of Christ's divinity and reality is not outward demonstration, but the contact of the heart with His living presence, through the Holy Ghost, as He reveals to us our sin, reads our inmost soul and makes Himself known to us in all His grace and glory.

## SECTION 48—TESTIMONY OF HIS LAST MIRACLE (John 21:1-9)

This is in some sense the most remarkable miracle of Christ's life for it is the only one performed by Him after His resurrection. It bears a strong resemblance, as we have elsewhere seen, to the first miracle of the draught of fishes three years before; but it is greater in every respect, especially in the spiritual lessons which it teaches us. While the former hinted at their calling to the imperfect service of their early apostleship, this foreshadowed their calling to the victorious service upon which they were now to enter in His resurrection life and power.

This glorious miracle was to them an impressive testimony to His reality and identity. John at once exclaims, as He recognizes the Master, "It is the Lord" (21:7). Peter, too, instinctively recognizes Him, and plunges into the sea to hasten to His feet, and afterward cries, in response to the Master's searching question, "Yea, Lord; thou knowest that I love thee" (21:15).

## SECTION 49—WITNESS OF JOHN (John 21:24)

The writer of this Gospel sums up all his long array of testimony by adding his own witness and then declaring that volumes more might have been written crowded with unpublished incidents of His grace and power.

## SUMMARY OF THE ABOVE TESTIMONIES

All these testimonies to Christ might be summed up under the following heads.

### 1. THE TESTIMONY OF HIS FATHER

This is given publicly at His baptism and again just before His crucifixion, both times in the hearing of the people. The third time, which John has not recorded, was on the Mount of Trans-figuration in the presence of the three disciples. Again and again, Jesus Himself appealed to His Father's witness as we have seen in the above references. How can we for a moment believe that God would witness thus to an impostor or to one whose claims were in any respect blasphemous or untrue?

### 2. THE TESTIMONY OF HIMSELF

This He had a perfect right to give. He constantly repeats it in the simplest and most impressive manner, showing in every case, and under the most solemn and difficult circumstances, that this was the deep and true consciousness of His whole being. This claim He constantly sustained in the most dignified and solemn manner throughout His whole life, not only in His discourses among both friends and enemies, but in the last awful scenes of His trial and agony, in the immediate presence of His Father and in the very hour of death itself. His calm assumption of divinity, and its perfect consistency and simplicity, is the divinest thing about the portrait of the Lord Jesus as given by John.

### 3. THE TESTIMONY OF SCRIPTURE

This, too, He applied in the face of His enemies. He claimed to be the Messiah of Moses and the prophets and based all His teachings upon their own Scriptures; nor were they able once to contradict or confound Him. All the details of His sufferings upon the cross are identified by the evangelist with Messianic prophecies. Indeed, it is as true of the Gospel as it is of the Apocalypse of John, that "the testimony of Jesus is the spirit of prophecy" (Revelation 19:10).

### 4. THE TESTIMONY OF JOHN

The witness of former prophets and Scriptures is summed up by the last of the Old Testament messengers, John the Baptist, in his own prophetic witness. Again and again did he declare, as the representative of the Jewish priesthood and the last voice of an-cient prophecy, that Jesus was the promised Messiah. The voice of the common people unanimously testified that "all things that John spake of this man were true" (John 10:41).

### 5. THE TESTIMONY OF HIS FRIENDS

To this we must add the witness of Christ's disciples and friends. We have in the first chapter of John the testimony of His earliest followers, Andrew, Simon, Philip and Nathaniel. We have it again in the witness of Nicodemus; the Samaritans; the nobleman of Cana; the blind man healed at Jerusalem; the disciples after His discourse at Capernaum; the multitudes who listened to Him in Jerusalem at the feasts; the faith and love of Mary, who anointed Him; the multitude who hailed Him as their king on His triumphal entry to Jerusalem; the testimony of Mary Magdalene, Thomas, Simon and John all combined in the one confession: This is He of whom Moses and the prophets did write; the Messiah, the Christ, the Son of the living God.

### 6. THE TESTIMONY OF HIS ENEMIES

The very officers who came to arrest Him acknowledged His wisdom and wonderful words. Caiaphas in the Sanhedrin confessed His power and even prophesied His atoning death. His accusers could say nothing against Him, and Pilate publicly vindicated Him even while he condemned Him.

### 7. TESTIMONY OF THE HOLY GHOST

We have seen how this witness was borne at His baptism and continually rested upon His spirit in all His teachings, supporting Him with marvelous wisdom and enabling Him always to meet His disciples and friends with divine love and grace. But after His departure, the blessed Comforter was to bear His highest and most impressive testimony to the glorious Master and His work. Ever since His Ascension, through His apostles and servants, there has been a succession of testimonies to the person and glory of Jesus.

### 8. THE TESTIMONY OF HIS OWN WORKS

He Himself appealed to this: "The works that I do in my Father's name, they bear witness of me. If ye believe not me, believe me for the very works' sake" (John 10:25, 38, author's paraphrase).

His first miracle in Cana was intended to show His own glory, and we are told His disciples thereafter believed on Him.

We have the record of many glorious miracles in John, every one of them bearing separate witness, as we shall see elsewhere, to some special phases of His work and glory and proving Him to be recognized by the omnipotence of God as divine. Not only were they works of power, but of the most gracious beneficence and the most tender and thoughtful love—ministering to vast multitudes of the suffering, drying the tear of the mourner and symbolizing the deepest and sublimest spiritual truths and blessings, they being signs as well as wonders.

# CHAPTER 3

# *LIFE IN THE GOSPEL OF JOHN*

THAT we might have life through His name is the great object of this little treatise.

This word, *life*, is the most pronounced keynote of the Gospel of John. Matthew teaches us of righteousness; Mark, of service; Luke, of mercy; but John opens the deeper fountains of the source of righteousness and the spring of service. We can trace the development of this beautiful evolution through twelve distinct stages and sections.

## CHRIST THE SOURCE

1. Christ is the source of life, and is Himself the life (1:4).

"In Him was life," or, as the same apostle expresses it in his Epistle, "This is the true God, and eternal life" (1 John 5:20). Life is not a thing, but a throb of His own heart in us.

## NATURAL LIFE

2. Natural life comes through Christ.

"All things were made by him; and without him was not any thing made that was made. In him was life; and the life was the light of men" (John 1:3-4). Creation is the outflowing of His life. Man's life and reason come from Him. He is the true Head of the natural creation, and He alone is worthy to be preeminent, and to be the Head of the spiritual creation.

## A NEW CREATION

3. He has come to bring us the life of a new creation which takes the place of the old life which has failed through man's sin and fall (chapter 2).

This is set forth in the miracle of Cana, the turning of the water into wine. The first wine at the marriage feast represents our natural life. The failure of the wine, before the feast was ended, vividly shadows forth the failure of human life and happiness through sin. The time comes in every experience when the cry goes forth, "There is no wine." The joys of youth and affection fade, and nature has no remedy. Then it is that the new wine of His love is revealed—not made in any measure from the wine of earth, but from the pure water of the Holy Spirit. Poured into the empty vessels of our hearts and bodies, it is richer, sweeter, purer far, than all the pleasures of earth, so that even the world says, when it truly tastes, "Thou hast kept the good wine till now."

This miracle is a parable of Christ's entire teaching and indeed of the gospel of His grace. Wine is the natural emblem of the deep, full pulses of life; and the blending of the two figures, the wine and the marriage feast, with its love and joy, constitutes the most vivid and expressive unfolding of the fullness of life and love in our consummated redemption.

## REGENERATION

4. The life of regeneration unfolding the spiritual meaning of this new wine (chapter 3).

The first stage of our spiritual life is regeneration. This is unfolded more clearly and completely in Christ's interview with Nicodemus than in any other portion of the Scriptures. The Jewish Rabbi had come to discuss the question of doctrine, but Jesus puts His hand upon his heart. He tells Nicodemus that what he must have is life. Until he possesses true heavenly life he cannot know aright or even see the kingdom of God.

This is not a matter of individual understanding, or even of moral character. It is a new-born life coming, definitely and divinely, from above—as real as the impartation of physical life to the newborn child. It is more, even, than the repentance and outward reformation which John the Baptist taught them and symbolized in their immersion in the Jordan. That is only being born of water. The life of which He speaks must be imparted directly by the Holy Spirit and be as truly a new creation as the divine touch which made the heavens and the earth, or in-breathed the physical life of man.

The outward senses cannot trace, and the understanding of man cannot penetrate, its mystery, even as we cannot comprehend the simplest form of physical life in the natural world. What it is we know not, although we may perceive its effects; and so of the deeper life of the Spirit it is true that it is wrapped in mystery, like the viewless wind, known only by its power and its results. "The wind bloweth where it listeth, and thou hearest the sound thereof, but canst not tell whence it cometh, or whither it goeth: so is every one that is born of the Spirit" (3:8).

Perhaps the greatest comfort implied in the beautiful teaching of the figure is that this birth begins at the lowest, weakest stage with the simple helplessness and feebleness of a babe. Let no one, therefore, despair, because he has not been born, like Adam, into full-grown manhood. If there is life enough for a cry, thank God, and praise Him for an infant's cry. Nicodemus, at this time, was scarcely even a babe, but the time came when he stood up with manly courage in the midst of the Sanhedrin to defend his Lord and even went to Pilate and begged His body for honorable burial.

The Lord then proceeds in the discourse that follows to show the manner in which this new life may be received. It flows from the eternal love of God in the gift of His Son that "whosoever believeth in him should not perish, but have everlasting life" (3:16). It is obtained by simply receiving and trusting Jesus who is Himself the life. This is the true secret of regeneration,

> But as many as received him, to them he gave power to become the sons of God, even to them that believe on his name: Which were born, not of blood, nor of the will of the flesh, nor of the will of man, but of God. (1:12-13)

All who thus receive the Saviour are quickened into His own spiritual life and become by birth the children of God; all who reject Him remain in condemnation with the added guilt of His rejection.

## INDWELLING LIFE

5. Indwelling life through receiving Christ into the heart (4:13-14).

In His conversation with the woman of Samaria the Saviour carries this thought farther and deeper. He reveals to her, for her thirsty and unsatisfied heart, the divine source of rest and pleasure which He had come to impart under the beautiful figure of the wellspring in the heart which the Holy Spirit gives to those who truly receive the indwelling Christ. The life becomes not now merely a draught of water, but a perennial fountain, an artesian well with its source in the soul itself, its supplies as lasting as eternity. This is more than regeneration; it is the fullness of Christ Himself, our life.

## ETERNAL LIFE

6. Eternal life through our deliverance from the law and judgment of God (5:24).

Here life is regarded in its judicial aspect as secured to the believer through the eternal decree of the righteous Judge, absolving forever from condemnation and preserving from future failure. It is not a mere probation, but it is a decree of life from the very Judge upon the throne based upon the redeeming work and unchanging Word of Jesus Christ. It delivers from death and even judgment all who receive it. Believing in His name we pass into a new world out of death into life and shall not come into judgment. He who is our Saviour is to be the future Judge. Accepting Him and saved by Him, we can stand without fear now and shall meet His coming without condemnation.

It is everlasting life for those who receive it. The judgment is already past, and the resurrection is already past in its spiritual and most immediate sense, for the dead have heard the voice of the Son of God and have come forth in a spiritual resurrection to die no more. Therefore, they need not fear the future call which shall raise the sleepers from the tomb, for that shall be the same voice which has already spoken through their souls to everlasting life. This life is inseparably linked with Jesus Himself. All who reject Him must inevitably lose it. Therefore, in closing this paragraph, His one complaint against His enemies is, "Ye will not come to me, that ye might have life" (5:40).

## THE LIVING BREAD

7. Spiritual and physical life day by day through vital union with Jesus (6:32-35, 47-51, 53-58, 62-63).

We have now come to the deeper waters of Ezekiel's river. They are waters to the loins. They touch the very springs of our entire being. Many of His disciples could not receive teachings so spiritual and profound. This discourse was the turning point in His Galilean ministry. From that time many went back and walked no more with Him.

Such teachings are still the turning point in the lives of many Christians. They require a closer union and more abiding fellowship with the Master than most people care for. He reveals Himself in this beautiful discourse as the very substance of His people's life. His flesh and blood give complete life for both body and spirit and are the true supply of our spiritual and physical need. After the resurrection, His living person, through the Holy Spirit, is to be the imparted life of all who dwell in Him. He distinctly points forward to His ascension, the revelation which the Holy Spirit is to bring and the time when all this is to be fully realized (6:62-63).

It is scarcely necessary to say that the Lord intended no such idea as that implied in the gross and literal doctrine of Roman transubstantiation. Even if they could eat the literal flesh of Jesus, it would be of no avail; but we can partake of the essence of His life and strength, imparted to our flesh by the Holy Spirit, as the subtle and yet supernatural force and vitality of our being. It is this that gives quickening and power to the spiritual life, and this is the true secret of divine healing; it is the life of Jesus made manifest in our mortal flesh. Thus He Himself lived upon His Father's life, and thus we are to live upon His. "As the living Father hath sent me, and I live by the Father: so he that eateth me, even he shall live by me" (6:57). Therefore, He could say in the temptation, when Satan tried to persuade Him to seek for physical strength from forbidden sources, speaking for us as well as Himself, "Man shall not live by bread alone, but by every word that proceedeth out of the mouth of God" (Matthew 4:4).

This, then, is the true ideal of Christian life, complete and continual dependence on the person of Jesus through the Holy Spirit for our entire life and strength; not only through outward and inward means of grace and strength, but personally and directly by the impartation of Himself. This requires the most intimate and uninterrupted communion with Him; therefore, He says, "He that eateth my flesh, and drinketh my blood, dwelleth in me, and I in him" (John 6:56). It is a union as close as that of the branches and the vine, the head and the body, the throbbing heart and its physical members, the mother and the babe that lives upon her very life.

## OVERFLOWING LIFE

8. The life overflowing in service for others (7:37-39).

Here we find the deep fountain of life running over the spring and finding vent in rivers of living water that go out to bless and save the world around us. It is beautiful to notice that as the blessing grows unselfish it grows larger. The water in the heart is only a well (in the fourth chapter); but when reaching out to the needs of others, it is not only a river, but a delta of many rivers, overflowing in majestic blessing.

This overflowing love is connected with the person and work of the Holy Spirit which was to be poured out upon the disciples after Jesus was glorified. This is the true secret of power for service—the heart filled and satisfied with Jesus and so baptized with the Holy Ghost that it is impelled by the fullness of its joy and love to impart to others what it has so abundantly received. Yet each new ministry only makes room for a new filling and a deeper receiving of the life which grows by giving.

## LIFE MORE ABUNDANTLY

9. Life more abundantly (10:10).

There are still deeper and richer experiences in the blessed Christ-life as the soul now passes into the experience of this precious chapter. Here we find ourselves in the fold of Christ.

In the intimacy of His discipline and love, He leads us in and out through richer pastures. He goes before us and makes us know His voice. He receives us into an intimacy with Himself, as close as His intimacy with the Father. He makes us know the meaning of His blessed covenant, "I give unto them eternal life; and they shall never perish, neither shall any man pluck them out of my hand" (10:28).

## RESURRECTION LIFE

10. Resurrection life (11:25; 12:24-25).

We now rise to the very highest teaching about our life in Christ. We come to the central principle of Christianity—death and resurrection. Not in the old natural sphere is this life perfected. Like the corn of wheat it must fall into the ground and die, or it abideth alone. Like Lazarus it must pass to the tomb and come forth again. Like the Lord Himself it must pass through the gates of death and come forth in union with His resurrection life.

This was the symbolical meaning of His baptism; this was the profound significance of the cross; and this is the very heart of all true spiritual experience. The life of nature, the strength of self-will, the affections of earth, the self-confidence of impulse, the ideas and opinions of the flesh, must all be laid down in the grave. We must come forth as those who are dead—our lives hid with Christ in God and drawn henceforth, each moment, from Him alone.

This was why Lazarus had to die, to foreshadow the greater resurrection. This was why the cup could not pass from Him, that it might bring the better resurrection. And this is why it is still true of all who follow Him, "He that loveth his life shall lose it; and he that hateth his life in this world shall keep it unto life eternal" (12:25). The two Greek words used here for life are different; the first signifying our self-life and the second our higher and everlasting life in Him.

## ABIDING LIFE

11. Life through abiding union and fellowship with Him (15:1-16).

We are now ready for the fullness of that personal communion which He had foreshadowed in the sixth chapter of John but between which and their actual experience lay the floods of death. These have now passed and the way is open for the fullness of His indwelling. There is a double union, "Ye in Me and I in you." The first secures our standing and justification, the second our quickening and deeper life.

The word *abide* expresses the habitual and moment by moment character of our walk with Him. Everything depends on the uninterruptedness of this life. It is simply a moment at a time, and Christ sufficient for that moment. The fruits of this blessed union and abiding are, first, our sanctification, "Now ye are clean" (15:3); second, our fruitfulness, "The same bringeth forth much fruit" (15:5); third, answered prayer, "Ye shall ask what ye will, and it shall be done unto you" (15:7); fourth, the Father glorified, "Herein is My Father glorified" (15:8); fifth, a consistent example before the world, "So shall ye be my disciples" (15:8); sixth, the fellowship of His love, "As the Father hath loved me, so have I loved you: continue ye in my love. If ye keep my commandments, ye shall abide in my love; even as I have kept my Father's commandments, and abide in his love" (15:9-10); seventh, the fullness of His joy, "These things have I spoken unto you, that my joy might remain in you, and that your joy might be full" (15:11); and eighth, His own personal friendship and intimacy, "Henceforth I call you not servants . . . but I have called you friends" (15:15).

## GLORIFIED LIFE

12. The perfection of our life in the glorious and final union of the whole body of believers in the Father and in the Son, in the unity of the church below, and through the ages of glory beyond (17:21-26).

These words express our Saviour's loftiest ideal for the life of His people. It should be one of perfect union with Him and the Father, even as He is one with the Father; not only thus in each individual, but the perfect union of the whole body of the believers together with each other and with Him. This should be realized even in the present life, for it is the Master's will and prayer for all His disciples. It will be the glory of the New Jerusalem and the perfection of the Bride. Even yet it will be fulfilled before the world, we believe, in such a manner that they shall believe that the Father hath sent Him. But its full realization is anticipated in the closing prayer, "That they may be with Me where I am to behold My glory" (17:24, author's paraphrase). Let us so live, and labor and pray that we may hasten the accomplishment of His dearest desire and hope for the church for which He died.

# CHAPTER 4

# *LIGHT IN THE GOSPEL OF JOHN*

THIS is another word which is very prominent and significant in the Gospel of John and one of the keynotes of its deeper teaching. We may trace it through almost the entire Gospel.

## 1. THE WORD

Christ as the Word, or primeval Light, manifesting and revealing God (1:1).

The very expression, "Word," suggests the idea of light. It is primarily the revealing of the thought of God. Christ is essentially light, inasmuch as He is God's expression to the universe of what He is Himself. The Epistle to the Hebrews calls Him "the outshining of the Father's glory, and the express image of His person" (1:3, author's paraphrase).

## 2. THE CREATOR

Christ, the Creator of nature and reason (1:4).

Physical light is the work of His hand. God said, "Let there be light: and there was light" (Genesis 1:3). This was the first act of the creating Word. So, also, the light of reason in man has all come from Him. "The life was the light of men" (John 1:4). The power of human thought, the understanding which men have used to deny God and dishonor Him, is a ray of divine intelligence.

## 3. OLD TESTAMENT LIGHT

Christ is the Light that shines in the Old Testament.

"He was in the world" (1:10); "the light shineth in darkness" (1:5). All the light of ancient revelation was but the radiance of the Sun of Righteousness. It was He who spoke to Abraham and Moses, and He was the Angel of the covenant in all the preparatory dispensations.

## 4. INCARNATE LIGHT

Christ has become the Light of the world through His incarnation (1:14-18).

In this glorious person we behold the Father's face and His beneficent character and purposes of grace toward sinful men. He is truly "A light to lighten the Gentiles, and the glory of thy people Israel" (Luke 2:32).

## 5. INNER LIGHT

Christ is the Light of those who receive Him, dispelling their doubts, and bringing to their hearts the light of faith and joy (John 1:38-49).

How beautifully we see this illustrated in the first disciples that followed Jesus. How promptly He answers their questions. How tenderly He receives them, instructs them and leads them to cry in glad assurance, "We have found the Messias" (1:41). "Rabbi, thou art the Son of God; thou art the King of Israel" (1:49). This is the light which brings its own evidence. It is enough to say to the questioning world, "Come and see."

This Christ is the light foreshadowed by the ancient types and prophecies. They could say of Him, "We have found him, of whom Moses in the law and the prophets, did write, Jesus of Nazareth, and the Son of Joseph" (1:45). He Himself could personally apply the glorious vision of Jacob's ladder and claim its fulfillment in His intercession which has opened heaven and restored men to fellowship with God.

## 6. THE REVEALER

Christ is the only Revealer of true heavenly light.

Verily, verily, I say unto thee, We speak that we do know,

and testify that we have seen; and ye receive not our witness. If I have told you earthly things, and ye believe not, how shall ye believe, if I tell you of heavenly things? And no man hath ascended up to heaven, but he that came down from heaven, even the Son of man which is in heaven. (3:11-13)

He, alone, had been in heaven and could bring to men the secrets of the unseen and unfold the will and love of His Father. Even as He spake He could say of Himself, "the Son of man which is in heaven." And what wondrous light He did reveal upon the character and love of God, lighting up the midnight interview with Nicodemus with a glory which has shone on millions of hearts and will continue to all eternity. That one sentence, " For God so loved the world, that he gave his only begotten Son, that whosoever believeth in him should not perish, but have everlasting life" (3:16), is worth a million times more than all the literature of the ages.

## 7. CONVICTION OF SIN

Christ is the Light that reveals sin.

And this is the condemnation, that light is come into the world, and men loved darkness rather than light, because their deeds were evil. For every one that doeth evil hateth the light, neither cometh to the light, lest his deeds should be reproved. But he that doeth truth cometh to the light, that his deeds may be made manifest, that they are wrought in God. (3:19-21)

The only reason, therefore, that people reject Him is because the light of His teaching condemns all sin and hidden evil that will not come to the light. It exposes their sin, only that it may lead them to the fount of cleansing which takes it all away.

## 8. SEARCHES HEARTS

Christ is the Light that searches and reveals the human heart.

"Come, see a man, which told me all things that ever I did: is not this the Christ?" (4:29).

Thus He searched this woman's heart and made her feel His

omniscience and divinity, and this drew her to Him for salvation.
So still His word is the mirror of human nature and makes every
convicted heart conscious of the searching eye of the Holy God.
"All things are naked and opened unto the eyes of him with
whom we have to do" (Hebrews 4:13), and yet amid all the
searching light we need not shrink from His eye for He searches
only to save.

### 9. INTERPRETER OF THE SCRIPTURES

Christ is the Light which explains the Scriptures.

"Search the Scriptures; for in them ye think ye have eternal
life: and they are they which testify of Me" (John 5:39).

The key to the Bible is Jesus. Its pages are obscure and dim until we learn to search in every part for His face of love and suffering. When we see Jesus, we have the key to all mystery and all
knowledge.

### 10. THE ONLY LIGHT

Christ is the only true Light.

Well might they ask, "To whom shall we go? thou hast the
words of eternal life" (6:68). There is no other name by which we
must be saved. "No man cometh unto the Father, but by me"
(14:6).

### 11. SATISFYING

Again, Christ brings the light of conviction and of consciousness to every obedient heart.

"If any man will do his will, he shall know of the doctrine,
whether it be of God, or whether I speak of myself" (7:17).

This is the divine criterion of truth and the remedy for doubt.
Truehearted obedience will always bring satisfying light and certain conviction that the teachings of Jesus are true and divine.
They must, however, be proved and practiced to be absolutely
known.

### 12. THE TESTIMONY OF HIS ENEMIES

Christ is the Light that transcends all human teachers; even in
the judgment of His enemies.

This was the testimony of the rude men who came without a thought of seriousness to fulfill their official functions as officers of the law; but they were captivated by the Saviour's wisdom and eloquence, and said, "Never man spake like this man" (7:46).

### 13. THE LAMPS IN THE TEMPLE

Christ is the Light of the world symbolized by the lamps of the temple, and shedding on the path of human life the direction and instruction required for all our practical needs. He is the Light of life, not only that leads to life beyond the grave, but our present life in all its perplexities and perils.

### 14. LIGHT AND LIBERTY

Christ is the Light that liberates us from the fetters of ignorance and sin.

"And ye shall know the truth, and the truth shall make you free" (8:32).

Slavery is often the result of mental degradation. Education and moral elevation often rescue the oppressed from human bondage, and spiritual light sets the soul free from the heavier bonds of sin and Satan. When we know our rights in Christ, and that Satan is a conquered foe, we spring into liberty and claim our true place as sons of God and freeborn citizens of the kingdom of heaven.

### 15. SIGHT

Christ is the Light that brings us vision as well as truth, sight as well as light.

This was beautifully illustrated by the healing of the blind man at Jerusalem (9:1-7). It was intended and used to emphasize the spiritual illumination He came to bring to benighted hearts, but which in their blind self-conceit the Pharisees refused to receive and so remained in deeper darkness (9:39-41).

### 16. GUIDANCE

16. Christ is the Light of personal guidance, step by step, in our daily lives (10:3-5, 14-15).

This is the light of His personal guidance; not merely a waymark, but a hand to lead the trusting disciple, and a voice that he cannot mistake if he is willing to be led. This is the light of which the psalmist sang, "I will guide thee with mine eye" (Psalm 32:8).

## 17. LIGHT BEYOND THE GRAVE

Christ is the only Light which shines beyond the grave.

"Jesus said unto her, I am the resurrection, and the life: he that believeth in me, though he were dead, yet shall he live; And whosoever liveth and believeth in me shall never die. Believest thou this?" (John 11:25-26).

Through this blessed promise the Lord has brought life and immortality to light through His own open grave. He has left the windows of glory forever open to the vision of faith and the souls of His departing saints.

## 18. TRANSIENT LIGHT

Christ is a transient Light which will soon pass away.

Touchingly is added this beautiful expression, "Jesus . . . did hide himself from them" (12:36), and so from those who reject Him the light has at length gone. The spirit of grace ceases to plead, and the soul does not have even light to know the meaning of its darkness and sorrow. Therefore, "while we have the light, let us believe in the light, and walk in the light, and be the children of the light" (12:36, author's paraphrase).

## 19. THE LIGHT OF JUDGMENT

Christ's word is the searching Light which will judge us in the last day (12:46-48).

The gospel of Jesus Christ, and the words which He has spoken, are to be the standard of future judgment. The manner in which we receive and obey them will determine our eternal destiny. The word which He has spoken to us, the same word will judge us in the Last Day. The very lamps of the throne are let down to shine upon our earthly path, and in the hour of the last assize they shall reveal our life and character. In some sense, therefore, every man may pass through His judgment here and may receive the conscious witness of the very authority which is at last to decide his fate.

## 20. THE HOLY SPIRIT

Christ has left us the Light of the Holy Spirit to continue and complete the teachings of His own personal life and work.

It is deeply interesting to trace the revelation of the Holy Spirit in the Gospel of John.

We see Him as He rests upon Jesus, the inspiration of all His teachings and the agent in all His supernatural works (1:33).

We see Him as the author of conversion in the individual soul. "Except a man be born of water and of the Spirit, he cannot enter the kingdom of God" (3:5).

We see Him as the indwelling fullness and overflowing life of the believer (7:38-39).

This, however, was an experience that was not to be fully realized until after Christ's resurrection, for we are told that the Spirit was not yet given because Jesus was not glorified.

We see Him revealed by Jesus as the Comforter who was to succeed Him—to complete His redeeming work in the hearts of His people and in the history of the Church.

a. The name by which He is revealed is beautifully expressive. It means "one called to us," or one on whom we may call in every emergency for instant and perfect help.

b. He was to be the substitute for Jesus, and at this stage of our experience to be even more to us than Jesus could be, for it was expedient for Christ to go away in order that He might come again. The physical presence of Christ could not be as internal and omnipresent as the Holy Ghost, who brings His actual life and presence into the depths of our being and to all the myriads of His people, irrespective of place or time.

c. He was to come in the name of Jesus, that is, the same Spirit that had dwelt in Jesus, and who still was to bring His personal presence and to be the medium of His indwelling life and personal revelation to the soul; so that when we have the Holy Spirit, we also have the presence of Christ.

d. He was to bring to their remembrance all things that Christ had said of Him and thus preserve and perpetuate the Master's teachings.

e. He was to reveal to them new truths which Jesus had not yet imparted because they were not yet able to receive them; the

Spirit would lead them into all truth (16:12-13).

f. He was to be more than a teacher but also a personal guide—not only teaching, but leading, disciplining and educating with a mother's tenderness the life and character of the disciples of Christ.

g. He was to unveil the future and complete the prophetic vision of the coming ages and the glorious appearing of the Lord Jesus in the end of the dispensation (16:13).

h. Above all else, He was to reveal Christ and testify to the person and character of Jesus Himself. "He shall testify of me" (15:26). "He shall glorify me, for he shall receive of mine, and shall shew it unto you" (16:14).

i. He was to "reprove the world of sin, and of righteousness, and of judgment" (16:8), using them as instruments and witnesses of the truth, but being Himself the effectual power by which the barriers of unbelief and sin were to be broken down and sinners convicted, comforted and led to Christ. Such was the glorious light that Jesus left behind Him as He passed within the veil; a light which still shineth in this dark world "until the day dawn, and the day star arise in [our] hearts" (2 Peter 1:19).

Once more we trace the revelation of the Spirit in this Gospel, as imparted by the risen Lord through the touch of His own living breath. He breathed on them and said, "Receive ye the Holy Ghost" (John 20:22), so that this blessed Spirit comes to us, not merely in His absolute Deity, but with the warm breath of Christ's living love, softened and humanized, if we may so speak, by passing through the medium of the Saviour's own heart and flesh. It is only as we get near enough to Jesus to feel the touch of His lips and the very kiss of His love, that we can receive the fullness of the Spirit's power. The impartation here described was for service and accompanied by the great commission, "As my Father hath sent me, even so send I you" (20:21). Though it was not fully realized until the day of Pentecost, it was in anticipation of that day that the words were spoken. But since Pentecost the Holy Ghost is already come. Each of us must receive His touch of fire and His enduing presence from the very lips and breath of our ascended Lord.

# CHAPTER 5

# *LOVE IN THE GOSPEL OF JOHN*

THIS is another of the emphatic words in this beautiful Gospel. It runs like a golden thread through almost every incident and utterance; like a majestic rainbow, it spans the heavens with its seven splendid tints of grace and beauty.

## 1. GOD'S LOVE TO THE SON

This shines out again and again and is implied in the beautiful phrase, "The only begotten Son, which is in the bosom of the Father" (1:18). He is not only the Son, but the Only Begotten; and His place is ever in the bosom of the Father's love.

Again, in John 3:35, it is declared, "The Father loveth the Son, and hath given all things into his hand." (See also 5:20-23.)

In John 6:57 He speaks of His intimate relation to, and dependence upon the Father, drawing His love every moment from Him, speaking His Word, fulfilling His law and supremely desiring to please Him.

Again He speaks of His peculiar dearness to His Father's heart, "He that sent me is with me: the Father hath not left me alone; for I do always those things that please him" (8:29).

In John 12:28 the Father bears public witness to His acceptance by a voice from heaven. Again and again, throughout the entire Gospel, He speaks of His absolute oneness and unceasing communion with the Father.

In John 16:27 He tells them that the very reason that the Father loves them is because they have loved the Son and believed upon His name. And, in His sublime prayer (17:5-26), He speaks of the glory which He had with the Father before the world was, and the love of which He has been the object from before the foundation of the world, and which love He asks for even them also. The veil is lifted from the most sacred and ineffable mystery in the universe, the heart of God, and the fellowship of the Father and of the Son. There is a unity and a love, of which all the highest forms of creature love are but as a drop to the ocean, and a spark to the sun. "God only knows the love of God."

There is yet one touch added to this picture in the account of the resurrection where Jesus, just emerging from the tomb, lingers a moment to comfort the weeping Mary Magdalene. He then hastens to lay His completed offering at His Father's feet, to receive His approval and welcome, before He can receive the touch of even His dearest friends. "Touch me not," He says to her, "for I am not yet ascended to my Father. . . . I ascend unto my Father, and your Father; and to my God, and to your God" (20:17).

## 2. GOD'S LOVE TO THE WORLD

"For God so loved the world, that he gave his only begotten Son, that whosoever believeth in him should not perish, but have everlasting life" (3:16).

Following the thought just expressed, this announces a mystery still more incomprehensible. It would seem as if the Father's love to His Son was for a moment outweighed by His love for the world. Inexpressibly dear as His beloved and only begotten Son was to Him, yet dearer was the salvation of His ruined children on this fallen earth. For them He spared not the treasure of His heart and the glory of heaven. Well may the apostle add, "He that spared not his own Son, but delivered him up for us all, how shall he not with him freely give us all things" (Romans 8:32).

This is not the only place in the beautiful Gospel of John where the Father's love to sinners is declared. Again and again Jesus announces that His coming is the Father's own act and purpose of love, and that redemption originated, not in His cross and incarnation, but in the ancient and everlasting mercy of our Father to ruined men. Very beautifully is this expressed in the following words:

I came down from heaven, not to do mine own will, but
the will of him that sent me. And this is the Father's will
which hath sent me, that of all which he hath given me I
should lose nothing, but should raise it up again at the last
day. And this is the will of him that sent me, that every
one which seeth the Son, and believeth on him, may have
everlasting life: and I will raise him up at the last day.
(John 6:38-40)

Back of all His words and works of love, Jesus ever recognized
the Father's coworking grace. Of His miracles of beneficence He
says, "My Father worketh hitherto, and I work" (5:17). Of His
people's security He declares, "Neither shall any man pluck them
out of my hand. . . . no man is able to pluck them out of my Father's hand" (10:28-29). Of our future reward He says, "If any
man serve me . . . him will my Father honor" (12:26). Of the
coming of the Comforter He declares, not only that He will send
Him, but that the Father will send Him in His name. His own
indwelling presence in our hearts is followed by the Father's love
and indwelling. "If a man love me . . . my Father will love him,
and we will come unto him, and make our abode with him."
(14:23). Not only does He love His disciples, but He assures
them that His Father loves them likewise, even with the same
love that He bears the Son. And thus the revelation of the Saviour's love coordinately reveals the love of the Father, too, and
His deep, divine, tender and everlasting interest in the salvation
of sinful men through the redeeming work of His dear Son. Indeed, Jesus, as a loyal Son, ever sought to glorify His Father's
grace and to teach His disciples to know and trust that Father's
perfect love.

## 3. CHRIST'S LOVE TO THE SINFUL AND LOST

It is difficult to select any single passage out of the many pictures of His grace and love to sinful men. One of the most beautiful of these is the story of His interview with the woman of
Samaria (4:4-26). The Bible contains no lovelier illustration of the
wisdom and love which sinful souls have shared. For this poor
sinner's sake "He must needs go through Samaria" (4:4). For love
of her thirsty heart He forgets His weariness at Jacob's well.

With unspeakable tenderness and delicacy He lays His hand first upon her aching heart and then upon the dark secret of her sin. When He has awakened her interest, her longing and her guilty conscience, then, with divine simplicity, He reveals Himself to her as her Saviour as well as the searcher of her heart. When the disciples come and ask Him to think a little about Himself and eat the food they brought Him, He explains Himself by telling them that the work of love in which He has just engaged is the meat and drink of His life.

Another touching and equally beautiful incident in this Gospel is of less certain authority as a part of the chapter where it occurs. It is the story of the woman taken in adultery (8:2-11). Still there is no reasonable doubt of its being part of the sacred volume and even of this Gospel. Yet it cannot properly be assigned to the place it occupies in the old version. It must have occurred at a later period, probably in the last week of the Saviour's life, in connection with the final conflict with the scribes and Pharisees in the temple; but these questions are of less importance than the spiritual teachings of this beautiful incident.

Here was a case of flagrant sin for which no excuse was offered. All the hostile use His enemies would make of any necessities of the situation, especially the leniency on His part toward her, seemed to demand that He should act with righteous severity, at least according to the strict letter of the law. By a stroke of infinite wisdom He silences her accusers in a moment and sends them from the room, more confounded than she, under the conviction of their own consciences. Then, by an act of sovereign grace, He forgives her sin without condoning or excusing it in the least degree. He dismisses her with the tender, solemn charge, "Neither do I condemn thee: go, and sin no more" (8:11).

One beautiful act of His delicate grace shines preeminent in all this incident. It was the refusal to look in the face of this poor woman while her accusers were present. Stooping down, He busied Himself writing on the ground, seeming to pay no attention to their bitter charges. This is the beautiful attitude which He still occupies in regard to His people's sins and the devil's charges against them. He listens as though He heard them not. "Who shall lay any thing to the charge of God's elect?" (Romans 8:33). But although He forgives, He forgives with a purity as beautiful as His grace is blessed, and speaks to her heart the solemn charge, which the truly forgiven never can forget, "Go, and sin no more" (John 8:11).

### 4. CHRIST'S LOVE TO THE NEEDY AND SUFFERING

No quality of the Saviour's character was more constantly manifested than that which Mark has expressed so often by the word *compassion*. We find many instances of it in the Gospel of John. We see it for the hungry multitudes in the wilderness (6:17). We see it in His coming to the toiling disciples in the tempest (6:19). We see it in His compassion for the poor cripple at Bethesda (5:6). We see it in His loving appeal to the multitudes at the Feast of Tabernacles. "If any man thirst, let him come unto me, and drink" (7:37). We see it in His compassion for the blind man (9:1-7), and in His gracious visit to this poor man when they had cast him out of the synagogue (9:35). We see it most beautifully of all in the story of Bethany and His love and tears at Lazarus' grave (11:17-44), revealing a heart that was as human as it was divine and that still is liable to be "touched with the feeling of our infirmities" (Hebrews 4:15).

### 5. CHRIST'S LOVE TO HIS OWN

The true place to know Christ's love is on His own bosom. The love of Jesus is known by His loved ones. Very tenderly and fully does John unfold his Master's love to His disciples.

a. The parable of the Shepherd and his flock (John 10:3-29).

He calls His own by name. He knows them intimately. He has a special voice for them alone. He leads them out gently by the hand. He always goes before them. He brings them into rich and abundant pastures. He stands in the place of danger. When the hireling flees, He defends them from the wolf. He gives His life for them. He holds them in His hand, so that they can never perish, nor any pluck them out of His hand or His Father's. He is indeed the Good Shepherd, fulfilling all the tender and gracious meaning which this figure had foreshadowed in all the utterances of the Psalms and prophets.

b. The picture of the home-circle at Bethany, where we have

an excellent picture of Christ's love to His personal friends with all the fine discriminations which personal friendships always unfold (11:5).

We know something from the other Scriptures of the faults of Martha, but, notwithstanding, she is first named in this picture of Christ's personal friendship. "Jesus loved Martha, and her sister, and Lazarus" (11:5). But this heavenly friendship has its strange tests, and, therefore, in the darkest hour of their life, the best friend they had seemed to fail them. Jesus lingered in the rear until Lazarus was cold in death and even corrupting in the grave. But His resources were, and still are, sufficient for every extremity. He came to them at last, not only to weep the tears of tender sympathy, which is often the best that human love can do; but, also, with His omnipotent love, to undo the work of death and give back to their arms the lost treasure of their affections. We have elsewhere pointed out the strange beauty of Christ's conversations with Martha and Mary, respectively. To the one He talks freely; with the other He only weeps. So, still, His love is exquisitely given to all His children's needs and temperaments, and His affection is as wise as it is strong and tender.

c. The picture of the washing of the disciples' feet (13:1-15).

This is the love that stoops to cleanse us from our defilements and to minister at our very feet. So, still, His blessed hands are daily cleansing and keeping our erring feet—stooping to depths of humiliation for us which we would not dream of doing for others. Not only with His hands, but with the very blood of His heart He ever keeps us cleansed from all sin. Well may we say with John in another place, "Unto him that loved us, and washed us from our sins in his own blood . . . be glory and dominion for ever and ever" (Revelation 1:5-6).

d. The last discourses and His parting words of love (John 14—16).

Volumes could not fully unfold the depths of love expressed in these divine words. How lovingly He comforts them. "Let not your heart be troubled" (John 14:1) He cries, when we might rather have expected them to say to Him, "Lord, let us comfort Thee." Then He promises them His personal comfort and deepest love if they will but obey Him. "He that hath my commandments, and keepeth them, he it is that loveth me . . . and I will love him, and will manifest myself to him" (14:21). This is the central thought in these, His parting words, that He is still to be linked with them by an unspeakable union and communion. He will so abide in them and they in Him, that His love shall flow into theirs, His peace shall be their peace, His joy their joy, His love their love and His works even shall be performed in them. All the power of His ascension glory shall be at their command for their necessities and their work.

e. His intercession for them (17:23, 26).

It is not merely that this one prayer for them exhausts His interest and love, for this is but a sample of the work on which He was just entering and which 1,800 years have not finished. Thus He still represents their interests at the Father's side. Whatsoever they ask in His name, He claims for them in His higher, priestly and all-prevailing intercession.

f. His great request for them that they shall be objects of the very same love which His Father has for Him (17:26).

Which of us would give away, or even share with another, the love of our dearest friend? This is the one thing that the human heart claims as its exclusive possession. There are some whose love we want supremely for ourselves, but Jesus gives to His disciples, and asks the Father to give to them, the very same love that He has for His beloved Son. We are received into His own actual sonship and take the place in the Father's heart which He Himself possesses. It is indeed unspeakable and prostrates our hearts in adoring wonder at His blessed feet.

g. His tender concern for their safety.

"If therefore ye seek me, let these go their way" (18:8). Here, even in the moment of His arrest, His thoughts are all for them. Offering His own body to His cruel enemies, He claims their exemption, just as He was about to offer His own body on the cross to all the horrors of the judgment which we deserved, and from which we have now exemption through His sacrifice and substitution.

h. His love to His mother on the cross (19:26).

This is a little gleam of human tenderness which shines the brighter because of the suffering through which He was at this moment passing. How it reveals His utter unselfishness, thoughtfulness and tender consideration for every human right and claim. What love it reveals on His part to His mother; how it honors the instinct of filial devotion in every human heart. What love it shows to the beloved disciple in the confidence reposed in his care and the trust committed to his keeping.

i. His love to Mary Magdalene (20:16).

One word expresses it all, and that one word her name. So still He speaks to the hearts that greatly love Him. There were some special reasons for His tender love to Mary; we love those best for whom we have done most, and she had been saved by His mercy. She, too, loved Him as perhaps few others ever loved Him. While Peter, and even John, had left the sepulchre without beholding Him, she could not and would not go until she had seen Him. Such persistent love He ever prizes and regards by the manifestation of Himself. If we would know all the fullness of His love, we must constrain it by a love that will not be consoled without Him.

j. His love to Thomas (20:27).

This is the pattern of His tenderness toward His questioning and doubting disciples. Still, often He makes us ashamed by the way in which He satisfies our doubts; let us rather, however, trust Him with the love that will not need to be reproved, even while its request is granted.

k. His love to Peter (21:15).

This represents His love to the backslider and His readiness to restore even the erring one who still loves Him; restore not only to His forgiveness, but even to the highest service, perhaps, all the more useful because of the lessons of humility it has learned through its own inconsistency.

l. His love to John.

One single expression tells the whole of this secret—an expression often repeated in this Gospel, "The disciple whom Jesus loved" (21:20). It is very beautiful to find John claiming this place for himself. Perhaps this was one reason why Jesus loved him, that, like a child, he claimed the tenderest love. He was not afraid to insist upon it and take it as unreservedly as the babe presses close to its mother's breast and assumes its right to all the love which it can claim. It is not necessary to say that such a babe is always the best loved. Jesus forbids none the closest place to His heart but loves us better the more closely we nestle to His bosom. John's place was one where we might well covet to lie, so near the Master's heart that he could know its very secrets, ask Him what others dare not, receive from Him the tender commission of service, write as no other could the record and unfold the mysteries of His divine character and His future kingdom and coming.

The Lord enables each of us to aspire to this high place and name, "The disciple whom Jesus loved who also leaned on His breast at supper" (13:23, 25, author's paraphrase).

## 6. OUR LOVE TO CHRIST

a. The absence of love is the fatal source of all sin.

"Ye are they which justify themselves before men; but I know you that ye have not the love of God in your hearts" (Luke 16:15, author's paraphrase).

b. The love of Mary (John 12:3).

Mary's gift was not only an expression of faith, but a sacrifice of love, teaching that Christ expects our personal affection and gifts for Himself. All that we do for the church and the poor can never be a substitute for His own personal claims.

c. Love is the condition of His indwelling (14:23).

It is to the loving heart that He loves to come and dwell, where He finds a welcome and a home. The root of piety is not intellect, but heart. Saintly souls are not cherubim, but seraphim, burning, rather than shining.

d. Love to Jesus makes us dear to His Father.

"For the Father himself loveth you, because ye have loved me, and have believed that I came out from God" (16:27).

e. The best proof of love is obedience.

"If ye love me, keep my commandments" (14:15). "If a man love me, He will keep my words" (14:23). "He that loveth me not keepeth not my sayings" (14:24). "If ye keep my commandments, ye shall abide in my love" (15:10). "Ye are my friends, if ye do whatsoever I command you" (15:14).

f. Love to Jesus is the best medium of spiritual revelation. The hearts that loved Him best were the quickest to recognize Him

(20:16; 21:7).

Mary Magdalene saw the Lord first, because her love would not let her go away. With weeping eyes and willing hands she waited at the grave, ready to bear in her own arms His dear body, out of the way of those who she supposed had removed it from the sepulchre. To such a heart, Christ is ever near; and the tear of love, like a heavenly lens, is quick to reveal His presence. John, too, through the mist of the Galilean morning, instantly knows his beloved Lord. It is the instinct of love, and he has finely expressed it by the beautiful words in his Epistle, "He that loveth not knoweth not God; for God is love" (1 John 4:8). "He that dwelleth in love dwelleth in God, and God in him" (1 John 4:16).

g. Love is the true impulse of service (John 21:15-17).

Christ is still asking, "Lovest thou Me?" of every worker before He commits to their hands His lambs, His sheep or His feeble suffering ones. No one is qualified to minister in His name without love. She is the queen of all the graces, and the greatest of all the gifts. Burning glasses can be made of ice and will set on fire the object on which they are concentrated, but hearts can be kindled only by hearts that are themselves on fire.

> "It needs the overflow of heart
>    To give the lips full speech."

## 7. LOVE TO ONE ANOTHER

This is the new commandment of the ethics of Jesus and the Gospel of John.

It was promulgated, not at Sinai, nor even in the sermon on the Mount, but at the supper table. The Mosaic law of love was, "Thou shalt love thy neighbor as thyself" (Leviticus 19:18); but the New Testament commandment transcends it, as far as the heaven is above the earth. "Love one another, as I have loved you" (John 15:12).

This is impossible for human nature. Such love must be itself divine; and is, indeed, nothing less than the very indwelling of the heart of Christ in our breast. Therefore, love in the New Testament is always recognized as a divine gift. Its very name, Charity, has the same root as the word "grace." It is a grace, and the gift of the Spirit of God.

One of the most devoted ministers of the Evangelical Church of France was a Rationalist in the beginning of his ministry. A neighboring pastor, who was evangelical and a most godly man, had long prayed for his conversion. One day he invited him to preach in his pulpit on the subject of love, the text being "Thou shalt love the Lord thy God with all thy heart, and thy neighbor as thyself." As he began to preach, the Holy Spirit brought to his heart, with irresistible conviction, the sense of his own inability to love according to the divine standard. Standing in the pulpit, with the tears running down his face, he confessed to his congregation that the love of which he had been preaching to them was something he did not possess and could not, himself, produce. Then there flashed upon his soul, by the same blessed convicting Spirit, the thought of Christ as the one who had come to do for us what the law could not do—not only to atone for our failure to meet the divine standard, but also to work in us the love which nature could not originate. And he began to preach, for the first time in his life, the gospel of Jesus Christ.

This, and this alone, must ever be the spirit of love. It is "the love of God shed abroad in our hearts by the Holy Ghost which He hath given to us. For when we were yet without strength (even to love), in due time Christ died for the ungodly" (Romans 5:5-6, author's paraphrase).

# CHAPTER 6

# FAITH IN THE
# GOSPEL OF JOHN

THIS is one of the keynotes of the Gospel as stated by the author himself. "These are written, that ye might believe that Jesus is the Christ, the Son of God; and that believing ye might have life through his name" (20:31).

## 1. THE TOUCHSTONE

We see it in the very beginning of the Gospel as the touchstone that separates between His friends and foes and divides all men into two great irreconcilable classes. Of the one it is said, "his own received him not"; of the other, "As many as received him, to them gave he power to become the sons of God" (1:11-12). Faith lifts us into the very family of God and becomes the gate of heaven, and unbelief excludes even the chosen people from any share in their inheritance.

## 2. THE FIRST DISCIPLES

We see the faith of the first disciples resting on the message of John the Baptist and afterwards on the personal testimony of individual disciples. Andrew and John believe on the word of their master, the Baptist; Simon believes on the testimony of Andrew; and Philip and Nathaniel believe on the direct words of Jesus Himself.

## 3. THE FIRST MIRACLE

We see next the still bolder faith of His disciples in His divine character in consequence of His first miracle and the manifestation of His glory. "This beginning of miracles did Jesus in Cana of Galilee, and manifested forth his glory; and His disciples believed on him" (2:11).

## 4. THE EFFECT OF HIS MIRACLES

The faith of the common people of Jerusalem in consequence of His supernatural works at the Feast of the Passover (2:23).

Jesus, however, perceived the shallowness of a faith that merely rested upon the evidence of miracles. Therefore He did not place any permanent dependence upon these people, for He knew what was in man. We see the same kind of faith in Nicodemus himself when he first came to Jesus and was faithfully taught the necessity of a deeper life than that of mere intellectual conviction.

## 5. SAVING FAITH

The Lord Jesus unfolds the deeper meaning of faith in His conversation with Nicodemus as the condition of everlasting life, through which we receive Christ and spiritual life through Him. Here faith is presented with the most solemn emphasis as the sole and imperative condition of salvation, and unbelief as the cause of condemnation and eternal ruin (3:15, 18).

## 6. THE RESULT OF KNOWLEDGE

The faith of the Samaritans, founded upon their own personal acquaintance with the Lord and His heart-searching revelation of their souls, and His own grace and love (4:29, 41, 42).

The woman of Samaria believed because she felt in her inmost soul that He had searched her heart and was no other than her Lord and Maker. He was, therefore, abundantly able to become her Saviour. Her neighbors gave their own independent testimony. They, too, had believed Him, not through her word merely, but through their own personal acquaintance with Him. True faith must ever rest upon our own knowledge of the Saviour. We must be able to say, "We have heard him ourselves, and know that this is indeed the Christ, the Saviour of the world" (4:42).

## 7. FAITH IN HIS WORD

The faith of the nobleman of Capernaum, resting on the naked word of Christ (4:47-50).

Jesus had felt that much of the faith hitherto manifested had been based only on His miraculous power. He, therefore, determined to lead this soul to the higher place of naked faith in His own simple word. Therefore He refuses any sign and complains that the people are abusing His very miracles by resting on them rather than on His word. Then, testing this man's faith by a bold promise, He bids him go forth without any other token of His child's healing than His own simple word. The man rises to meet his test and dares to believe the simple promise of the Saviour. He goes his way to find it literally fulfilled, teaching us, through all time, the simplicity of faith and the instantaneous results which it will ever bring.

## 8. CLAIMING ETERNAL LIFE

Faith delivering from condemnation and claiming eternal life (5:24).

This mighty word has power to cancel the very curse of the law, to turn back the fiery work of judgment and to open the portals of immortal life to the soul that dares to claim it.

## 9. HINDRANCES OF FAITH (5:44).

These, He shows them, are mainly a spirit of worldliness and a subserviency to the opinions of men. This is fatal ever to true faith in God; indeed, any unholy condition must always be fatal to true faith. In a previous verse He intimates that their own willfulness was the cause of their rejecting Him. "Ye will not come to me, that ye might have life" (5:40).

## 10. LIVING BY FAITH

Faith receiving Jesus as the Bread of Life for our souls and bodies (6:35).

Not only does faith secure our future salvation, but it enters into the fullness of Jesus for our present needs. This the Galileans could not and would not receive; and this, today, is equally incomprehensible and offensive to the majority of professing Chris-

tians. A life of faith upon the Son of God, and the habit of trust-
ful dependence upon Him for the nourishment of our spirits and
the health of our bodies, is regarded as the foolishness of mysti-
cism and sentimentalism; but to those who thus know Him, it is
the very balm of life, the bane of care and sorrow and the secret
of the Most High.

## 11. FAITH TESTIFYING

Faith testifying to Christ (6:68-69).

As we have already seen, this testimony was called forth by
the withdrawal of the great majority of Christ's Galilean followers. Peter and his brethren did not yet fully understand all
that the Master's profound teachings had meant, but they believed and received as far as they could. Their own experience,
in its true form, expresses more than one beautiful truth, "We
believe and know for ourselves that Thou art the Christ" (6:69,
author's paraphrase). These are the two stages of faith: first we
believe, and then we know by actual consciousness and heart-
satisfying experience the truth of these precious promises.

## 12. RECEIVING THE HOLY GHOST

Faith bringing us into the fullness of the Spirit (7:38).

We have already referred to this promise of the overflowing
fullness of the Holy Ghost. Here it is connected with believing;
thus, only can we ever receive the Holy Ghost. We must expect
to accept Him, trust Him and treat Him as having fully come.
Moses was commanded to speak to the rock and it would flow
forth, but not to strike it in any doubt or uncertainty (Exodus
20:70-12). So, still, the whisper of trust ever brings the fullness of
blessing.

## 13. THE LIFE OF FAITH

Believing and continuing (John 8:30-32).

Here we find the Lord encouraging the disciples, who had taken
the first steps of faith, to continue in His word and pass on into all
the fullness of spiritual freedom and conscious experience of the
truth. So faith must ever be rooted and grounded and built up in
Him, for "we are made partakers of Christ, if we hold the begin-

ning of our confidence steadfast unto the end" (Hebrews 3:14).

### 14. THE BLIND MAN

The faith of the blind man (John 9:35-38).

We have here a beautiful example of the beginning of faith. This man had followed all the light he had and had fully confessed it as he received it. Healed by the Lord, he had briefly and constantly borne witness to Him in the face of persecution until at last he had been excommunicated from the synagogue for Christ's sake. Then the Lord met him and led him into fuller light, as He ever does the soul that uses all the light it has. And as the new light came, he accepted it without reserve, believing and worshiping his Lord and becoming a monument of that simplicity which has often put to shame the pride and unbelief of the world's boasted wisdom.

### 15. MARTHA

The faith of Martha (11:22, 27, 40).

We have here a very remarkable example of faith. Martha's heart had sunk when she saw her brother die and the Master fail to come. For a moment she reproached Him with the neglect (11:21), but then there rises in her heart a sudden gleam of hopeful expectation that even yet it is not too late for His almighty power to remedy the disaster. "I know," she says, "that even now, whatsoever thou wilt ask of God, God will give it thee" (11:22).

This was undoubtedly a literal intimation that even Lazarus could be raised from the dead. The Lord encourages it and reveals Himself as the One who possesses, in Himself, all the powers of resurrection life. He more than hints His consent to her amazing request. "Thy brother shall rise again" (11:23).

For a little Martha does what we all do at such times; she drops down her faith a little and slips it forward into the future. "I know that he shall rise again in the resurrection at the last day" (11:24). Jesus meets her retort by holding her to the present moment and to His own sufficiency. "I am the resurrection, and the life" (11:25), He replies.

Poor Martha does not quite meet the issue with definite present assurance, but she rolls her burden over upon Him and rests in Himself as the almighty Son of God and the promised Messiah. "Yea, Lord: I believe that thou art the Christ, the Son of God, which should come into the world" (11:27).

He must have read in her words a deeper faith than she expressed, and He evidently felt it essential that she should stand fast in this faith. This is one of the conditions of the miracle that He is about to perform, for He adds a little later, when she expressed concern and doubt about removing the stone because Lazarus was so long buried, "Said I not unto thee, that, if thou wouldest believe, thou shouldest see the glory of God?" (11:40).

Therefore the resurrection of Lazarus was, in some measure, connected with the faith of Martha. But there was a mightier faith than Martha's. He is still the faith as well as the power in all His words of omnipotence through His trusting children. How calm and lofty is the confidence of that marvelous prayer, "Father, I thank thee that thou hast heard me. And I knew that thou hearest me always" (11:41-42). So, still, He waits to work and believe in us.

### 16. MARY

The faith of Mary (12:3, 7).

This, at first, looks like an act of love, but deeper than love was the root of faith from which it sprang. This is revealed in the seventh verse by the testimony of Jesus concerning her. It was because she knew that He was about to die as her suffering Saviour, that Mary had kept this costly ointment. Now she comes with hands of loving faith to set Him apart for the altar of sacrifice. She had an intelligent appreciation of His character and work which perhaps no other of His disciples in any such measure shared. So, still, the faith which best understands the cross of Calvary will most effectually work by love and lay the richest and costliest offerings at His feet.

### 17. TIMID BELIEVERS

Faith that fears to confess Jesus (12:42-43).

In contrast with Mary we see here another kind of faith which has plenty of counterparts in the Church today; a faith which has no doubt of Christ's divinity and Messiahship, but dares to go only as far as is consistent with worldly interest and reputation for it loves the praise of men more than the praise of God. Jesus challenges all such cowardly hearts to the bar of God. He appeals to the hour when they shall stand in the judgment and find that to have confessed Jesus amid reproach and shame was to have stood for God and won His acknowledgment when all other faces shall be covered and one smile from Him will be worth a thousand worlds.

## 18. BELIEVE ALSO IN ME

Faith in Jesus Himself as a divine person, equal with the Father, and as the very expression and image of the Father (14:1, 10, 11).

The Lord Jesus seeks here to link their faith in Him with all that had been sacred in their conceptions of God, and to assume to Himself as the object of their confidence, all the majesty and fullness of all previous revelations of the Father. "Ye believe in God, believe also in me" (14:1). What a softened light this sheds upon the name of God and the glory of His majesty, and what a majesty it sheds upon the name of Jesus. They had learned to trust His love; they must now add to this the conception of His transcendent, infinite power and Godhead. So our faith in Him must recognize His divine glory.

## 19. FAITH AND POWER

Faith in Christ as the secret power for our Christian work (14:12).

Not only must they believe in His union with the Father, but they must likewise believe as fully in their union with Him. The works they are to do are not to be their works, but His works in them. As He is now entering upon a higher stage of His mediatorial work, they must expect to be the channels and instruments of even greater power than they have yet witnessed, even in His ministry. But the vital link of this power must ever be a living faith, a faith that receives Him constantly to work His own works in them and dares to expect Him to do even greater works than in the days of His flesh. Do we thus believe in Him, does He thus work in us, are our works His work and does He work the greater works in our lives?

## 20. FAITH AND PRAYER

Faith as the condition of effectual prayer (15:7-16).

Faith is expressed in these passages by abiding in Him and asking in His name, that is His very character, as if He Himself were asking. This is true faith, to identify ourselves with Jesus, and pray with His rights and claims. Such prayer will ever be in accordance with His will and must prevail.

## 21. FAITH IN THE RISEN SAVIOUR

Faith in the risen Saviour (20:8-16).

The first to believe in the resurrection was John. The beauty of his faith was that it was immediate, implicit and without waiting for visible evidence other than God had already given. He saw and believed. He saw not yet the Lord, but he saw enough to rest his faith upon and to recall to his mind the previous words of his Master which he, with the others, had forgotten. No doubt, his faith now rested on the recollection of the simple promise which Jesus had made before His death and which he refers to in the next verse (20:9). Mary's faith was different. It was the result of a personal manifestation of Christ. It was inspired by His own living voice; and thus, in both these cases, faith rested on the Saviour's words.

## 22. THOMAS

The unbelief of Thomas, and the lesson it teaches us of the highest faith (20:24-29).

The other disciples all believed on the testimony of those who had seen the Lord. Thomas refused to be satisfied with less than a complete series of tests. He was a regular materialist and wanted signs and evidences to rest his faith upon. The Lord condescended to give him what he demanded; but when it came, there came also the higher witness of Christ's own presence and His searching revelation of Thomas' unbelieving heart so that he did not now need the visible sign. Thomas threw himself at the Master's feet, exclaiming in the language of irresistible conviction and unconditional submission, " My Lord and my God" (20:28).

Jesus takes occasion from this to teach the great truth which He had hinted at in the beginning of the Gospel in connection with the healing of the nobleman's son. The true resting place of faith is not material signs, but the word of Jesus Himself. He pronounced the lasting benediction which it is possible for every one of us to obtain. "Blessed are they that have not seen, and yet have believed" (20:29).

## 23. FAITH IN THE WORD

Faith resting on the written Word (20:31).

It is the record which the Holy Ghost has "written." "These are written, that ye might believe" (20:31). This is the great truth which John unfolds so simply in his Epistle. "If we receive the witness of men, the witness of God is greater: for this is the witness of God that He hath given us eternal life, and this life is in His Son. He that believeth not the record hath made Him a liar. These things have I written unto you that believe in the name of the Son of God; that ye may know that ye have eternal life" (1 John 5:9–11, 13, author's paraphrase). By believing the record, therefore, which God has given of His Son, we know that we have eternal life. And then we receive the second witness in ourselves, His Holy Spirit, and the peace and joy He brings into the believing soul.

## 24. DEVELOPMENT OF FAITH

It is interesting to trace the development of faith and unbelief in the Gospel of John on the part of His friends on the one side, and His adversaries on the other.

In the first four chapters we trace the gradual development of faith. First, we have the inquiries of the priests and Levites made of John the Baptist (1:19) and showing considerable interest.

Next we see the open adherence of some of John's disciples, as they leave him to follow Jesus (1:37).

Next we find Philip and Nathaniel, two typical Galileans, joining the little band of new disciples (1:43-49).

In the second chapter the manifestation of Jesus becomes more marked and the faith of His disciples more pronounced. "This beginning of miracles did Jesus in Cana of Galilee, and manifested forth his glory; and his disciples believed on him" (2:11). From Galilee the scene is changed to Jerusalem, and there we see the steady development of faith in Him.

First, among many of the common people (2:23).

Next, in the spirit of earnest inquiry in Nicodemus (chapter 3).

And then in the wide extension of His Judean ministry in the country where many became His disciples. And His ministry grows larger and wider even than John's (4:1-2).

The development still goes on, removing from Judea to Samaria (chapter 4), where we see the remarkable faith of the Samaritans. It finally culminates in the strong faith of the nobleman of Capernaum (4:46-54).

## DEVELOPMENT OF UNBELIEF

We now come to the second series in this development, namely, the manifestation of unbelief on the part of His enemies (chapter 5) in connection with the healing of the impotent man. Its issue is summed up in the Lord's words: "Ye will not come to me, that ye might have life" (5:40).

In the sixth chapter, the conflict changes to Galilee. It speedily terminates, in the close of that chapter, by His rejection on the part of the Galileans on account of His deeper spiritual teachings and His refusal to enter into their ambitious project to establish an earthly kingdom (6:66). The Galilean contest is now over, and the scene again changes to Jerusalem in the seventh and eighth chapters.

We have His disputations with them at the Feast of Tabernacles, ending in their attempt to stone Him (8:59).

The next conflict is at the Feast of Dedication, three months later, and it is closed with a similar attempt (10:39) and his retirement to Bethabara (see 10:40 and 1:28).

## HIS GLORY MANIFESTED AND BELIEVED

The series closes with His supreme manifestation of His power and glory, in the resurrection of Lazarus, and the final and determined plot of the entire Sanhedrin to destroy Him which led, soon after, to His crucifixion.

Each of these stages of unbelief and hostility on the part of His enemies is characterized by corresponding faith on the part of His friends. Over against their rejection in chapter 5 is the faith of the impotent man at Bethesda's pool. In contrast with the rejection of the Galileans is the confession of Peter and the disciples (6:68-69). The unbelief of the rulers, at the Feast of Tabernacles, is met and confounded by the faith of the poor blind beggar (chapter 9). The mad and reckless opposition aroused by the resurrection of Lazarus stands out in bolder relief from the faith and love of Mary and Martha (chapters 11 and 12) and the enthusiasm of the common people (chapter 12), as they publicly hail Him as the Son of David and the King of Jerusalem.

The final stage in this process of development of faith we see in the closing chapter of John, on the part of His disciples. Their perplexities and questionings come out most truthfully in the discourses at the table (13:36; 14:6, 8, 22; 16:18).

They enter into clearer light as He closes His address. "Now are we sure that thou knowest all things, and needest not that any man should ask Thee: by this we believe that thou camest forth from God" (16:30). Then comes the dark shadow of Peter's fall (18:27), followed and counter-balanced by the devotion of John and the brave women who still lingered around the cross (19:25-26), also the courage of Nicodemus and Joseph (19:38-40).

With the morning of the resurrection comes the faith of John himself (20:8), the joyful recognition of Mary (20:16), the confession of Thomas (20:28) and the restoration of Peter (21:15, 19), all summed up by the final testimony of John himself, as the foundation of our unfaltering faith through the coming generations.

# CHAPTER 7

# TEN INCIDENTS IN THE GOSPEL OF JOHN

W E find in this wonderful Gospel some remarkable incidents illustrating the grace, glory and character of Jesus.

## 1. VARIETIES OF CONVERSION

Interview with the first disciples, or the varieties of conversion
(1:29-51).

### THROUGH THE GOSPEL

We have here an illustration of the varieties of conversion. The
first of these disciples was led to Christ by the preaching of John
the Baptist. It would be well if all preaching were as definite and
evangelical. There would be more Andrews if there were more
John the Baptists. The great preacher knew that he was sending
away his own disciples, but he did not shrink from pointing them
to the greater Master. He was not ashamed to repeat the same
sermon the next day. This is a text in which no minister need
ever be ashamed to repeat himself. The story of the cross is a gospel that never grows old.

### THROUGH PERSONAL EFFORT

Andrew, like every true convert, becomes an evangelist, and
for the rest of his life the notices that we have of him represent
him in this aspect of helping others. In the present case, he first
finds his own brother and brings him to Jesus; so the second conversion here is through personal influence on the part of our own

immediate relatives. What a lesson it teaches us of our obligation to the souls of those who are nearest to us. Forever Andrew will be a partner of the fruits of Simon's life, for he brought him to Jesus.

The way he brought him was by his own personal testimony; the reason he was able to give so clear a testimony was that he himself had come so near to Jesus. He had not only gone to Him, but he had gone with Him. The whole previous day he and John had spent at home with the new Master—a wonderful type of that deeper fellowship which the converted soul may enter, and must enter, if it would be able to bring others to Christ.

### A DAY WITH JESUS

What a sweet picture of the soul's introduction to the Saviour. These two disciples had followed Jesus at the invitation of John, but no one ever follows Christ unnoticed. Turning around and recognizing them, He asks them a very simple but searching question, "What seek ye?" (1:38). If they had been seeking anything but Himself, the interview would have ended here; happily for them, however, that they could truly answer, "Rabbi . . . where dwellest thou?" (1:38). They did not have to wait for the welcome to His presence and His home; they went with Him and abode that whole day. Many a wondrous unfolding of heavenly truth entered their hearts as they waited the happy hours at His blessed feet.

So, still, He waits to receive His humblest disciples to abide. Peter is welcomed with no less frankness and simplicity. The Lord knows him from the beginning and intimates in His first words His honest opinion of Simon, the son of Jonas, the impulsive and unsteady man; but He also reveals the stronger qualities which are to come to him through the grace of God and make him the very rock cut out from the Rock of Ages which is to be one of the foundation stones of the Christian church.

### THE CALL OF JESUS

The next conversion in this group is through the direct call of Christ Himself. It is Philip of Bethsaida. He, too, responds immediately and becomes, in turn, like Andrew, a messenger to others. Afterward, along with Andrew, he is the instrument of bringing to Jesus the strangers in the temple who came to seek the Saviour.

### THE CALL OF A FRIEND

The last of this group of disciples was brought to Christ by the personal influence not of a relative, but of a friend. Philip found Nathaniel in return and brought him to Jesus. Nathaniel, however, was not willing to take so great a matter on the word of Philip; yet, like a wise man, was willing to come and see. As he met Jesus, a single sentence from Him made the old Israelite feel that he was in the presence of the searcher of his heart. Falling at His feet, Philip gave Him homage in the loftiest faith as the "Son of God" and "King of Israel" (1:49). Nathaniel was a true Israelite, a man of upright and blameless character, and yet even the highest morality needs something more, even the revelation of Jesus Christ and the spirit of childlike faith in the divine Saviour.

In these five disciples we have a beautiful picture representing, in miniature, the story of Christianity and the various ways in which, since then, Christ has been leading myriads of souls to himself.

## 2. NICODEMUS

Nicodemus, or the first inquirer (3:1-21).

We have already seen in this incident the spiritual teaching of the Lord Jesus with regard to the new life and the necessity of regeneration. We also may learn from it many precious lessons respecting Christ Himself and His method of dealing with souls. This man, like many other inquirers, came to talk and argue, but Jesus declined all speculations and questionings about even the truth. He threw Nicodemus at once back upon himself and his need of a radical change of heart. Indeed, He tells him that without a new spiritual nature his ideas and opinions are of no value for he cannot even see the kingdom of God until he is born again.

Nicodemus' first word was, "We know" (3:2). Most people, like him, are hindered by what they know. He represented the highest type of an ancient moralist and formalist, still destitute, however, of true spiritual life. Jesus' first step, therefore, is to humble him and show him his deep spiritual need, and His next to lead him sweetly to see in the gospel God's full provision for this need.

We should never preach regeneration apart from Christ and simple faith in Him. The true place to obtain a new heart is not by looking into our old one, or trying to improve it, but by bowing at the feet of Jesus and believing in Him as our sin-atoning Saviour.

### 3. SOUL–WINNING

The woman of Samaria, or the wisdom that winneth souls (4:5-30).

We have already referred to this incident in connection with the love of Christ for sinners. For a moment let us still glance at it as a lesson in soul-winning.

The first thing that strikes us about it is the incidental character of His work in saving this woman. It was one of those opportunities which come to us constantly by the way and which He was always ready to meet and improve. Much of our best work should be unstudied and spontaneous.

The real secret of His usefulness in this and in every case, was His intense love for souls. He could truly say to His disciples, "My meat and drink is to do My Father's will and work" (4:34, author's paraphrase). Work like this was His very life and joy. And so, if we are to win souls, it must be our delight, and we must be watching for them. The literal translation of the word *receiveth sinners* is, "this man lieth in wait for sinners."

We see also in this case the finest tact in His interesting the woman before He attempts to impress her. He awakens her interest and confidence by meeting her in an easy and friendly manner and asking a little favor of her. He stooped to her level and even surprised her by His entire freedom from all the prejudices which she expected from a Jewish Rabbi. If we would save people, we must come near them. The earliest Moravian missionaries to the West Indies became slaves that they might win the confidence of the degraded natives.

Then He awakens her curiosity and spiritual hunger by hinting at the needs of her own sad heart and the blessings He is able to give in return, if she but knew. There is always a sore place in every human heart that a loving hand can touch and find in it a point of contact with the gospel. To speak of the living water is often enough to awaken the thirst.

### HER CONSCIENCE

But there is a deeper need, and that is her sin. It would not do to tell her of it, for this might offend her; she must see it herself. And so a simple question, "Go, call thy husband" (4:16), becomes the occasion of awakening her conscience and bringing from her lips the frank confession that lays her poor guilty heart at the feet of the Saviour. But now she tries for a moment to turn aside and evade her conscience and the leadings of God's Spirit by a spirit of controversy about the difference between Jewish and Samaritan worship.

### REVELATION OF JESUS

The Master refuses to enter into the controversy farther than to use it to awaken her own sense of God's spirituality and her need of a personal acquaintance with Him in her secret heart. She feels the lack of this, and her soul instinctively cries out for someone to lead her to God. She exclaims, "I know that Messias cometh, which is called Christ . . . he will tell us all things" (4:25).

She had been led thus, step by step, up to the very portals of faith. All that is necessary now is to draw aside the veil and reveal Himself to her heart. No human language can express all that is meant in that little sentence that follows, "I that speak unto thee am he" (1:26). We must go back to the moment when He revealed Himself to us, to understand it.

It is proper that a curtain should here fall upon the scene and she be left with the secret of her new and eternal joy. She is saved, she has found her Lord, but she cannot keep the secret. She, too, in turn, becomes a messenger of love to bring her countrymen to the same wondrous Teacher that has searched and saved her own soul.

## 4. THE SINFUL WOMAN

The sinful woman, or the mercy that pardons without palliating sin (8:2-11).

We refer elsewhere to the critical question connected with this passage; here it is enough to see in it the heartless severity of weak man toward sin in others in contrast with the tenderness and long-suffering of Christ to the erring. These Pharisees were, by their own confession, as impure as this poor woman, and yet they could drag her forward into shameful exposure and without a touch of mercy demand her instant death and all the eternal ruin it must bring. Jesus, on the other hand, with an infinite hatred of sin and free from a spot or stain of defilement, could see deeper than her sin and feel the tenderest compassion and mercy toward the poor sinner, while He gave no indulgence or countenance to the sin.

What a lesson we also learn about the necessity of our own blamelessness if we would sit in judgment upon others. When we are without sin, then we can cast the stone of censoriousness at our fellows and have "a readiness to revenge all disobedience, when [our own] obedience is fulfilled" (2 Corinthians 10:6). What a beautiful example we learn of being blind to the faults of others when in the presence of the accuser. While they were talking against this poor woman, Jesus wrote upon the ground as though He heard them not. Happy for us all if we had thus learned to listen to the backbiting tongue.

How vividly the power of conscience appears in the presence of innocence. One look from His honest face into their hearts, and they felt all their secret sin exposed. They hurried from His presence to hide themselves from their own consciences and His searching gaze.

*HIS DELICACY*

Jesus dealt with this poor woman, too, but He deals with her alone. Not in the presence of others can we tell the soul of its faults, nor when it feels we have listened to evil reports or unfriendly tongues. How beautifully He preserved the confidence of this poor heart by His manly and lofty sensitiveness to her feelings, refusing even to look in her face or see her blush of shame while her enemies were near. Only when they are alone He looks into that weeping countenance and speaks the word of mercy and yet of faithfulness. Christ's first word to her is forgiveness, free and full, not founded upon her innocence or promises of amendment, but springing only from His own undeserved grace. But His next word is a word of infinite holiness, "Go, and sin no more" (John 8:11). "There is forgiveness with thee, that thou mayest be feared" (Psalm 130:4).

There is no such remedy for sin as love. "We have tried everything to reform Him," said the Duke of Wellington about a deserter they had punished till it seemed vain. "It is useless; there is nothing left but to execute him." "Please your highness," said a poor soldier, "there is one thing you have never tried." "What is that?" asked the duke. "Please your highness, you have never tried forgiving him." And so it was tried, and not in vain, for the hardened deserter became the noblest and truest heart of all the soldiers of the Peninsula.

## 5. MARY OF BETHANY

The anointing at Bethany, or the preeminence of love (John 12:1-8).

This beautiful incident is the highest expression of love to Jesus that we meet with during His earthly life.

We have already seen that it was from one who best of all understood the meaning of His death, and that it was an act of faith quite as much as a gift of love. It was this that inspired Mary's love, that she understood so well that He at whose feet she sat with delight was about to die for her. And so our love must still draw its inspiration from the cross. But the chief lesson of this scene is that Jesus appreciates and requires our personal and highest love directly for Himself.

Judas, like many people still, thought that the ointment was wasted because it had not been given to the poor, but Christ replies that there is something even more than giving to the poor, namely, the offering that is placed directly at His feet and offered only to Himself. Each of us has a vessel we can break and a fragrance we can pour at those sacred feet, namely, our own heart with all its treasures of love.

It is possible to do much work, and even give all our goods to feed the poor, and yet be strangers to true love to Jesus. Nothing can be a substitute for love to Jesus. The very perfume of Christianity has ever been the incense of fervent pity and personal love to Christ. The world may call it waste, but Jesus treasures it in vials full of odors sweet before the throne.

## 6. HUMILITY

Washing the disciples' feet, or the humility that springs from true greatness (13:1-10).

The first lesson taught by this picture is that of Christ's humility. Like Him, we cannot truly stoop until we have learned our high calling and know that we are indeed the sons of God. Then we shall not fear the most menial service or think that the lowliest place can degrade our true dignity. We shall prove that we are the chief by becoming the servant of all.

The next lesson is love, that, instead of exposing the stains of one another, seeks to wash them away. But the deepest spiritual teaching of these words is the unfolding of Christ's own constant cleansing as our ever living Advocate and High Priest. Still He is girded with the towel, and still He stoops to cleanse the stains of defilement from our feet day by day.

### CLEANSING

This is not the act of justification by which He forgives the sinner, but it is the constant keeping of His own disciples. Two expressive words are used in the passage for cleansing; the first, *Luo*, signifying a complete washing of the whole person; the second, *Nipto*, meaning a partial washing, as the feet. The first of these, He says, does not need to be repeated. Once for all they have been justified, but day by day they need to be thoroughly and constantly cleansed from the travel stains of the way.

The tense used for the first is the perfect tense, "He that hath been bathed (in his justification) needeth not save to wash his feet, but is clean every whit" (13:10, author's paraphrase). In the first chapter of his beautiful Epistle, John has taught the same truth in the words: "If we walk in the light, as he is in the light, we have fellowship one with another, and the blood of Jesus Christ his Son [keeps cleansing] us from all sin" (verse 7). "If we confess our sins, he is faithful and just to forgive us our sins, and to cleanse us from all unrighteousness" (verse 9).

## 7. HIS MOTHER

The message concerning His mother, or the humanity and divinity of Christ (19:25-27).

Of course, the first thought suggested by this exquisite picture is the love of Jesus to His mother and the enduring example which exalts filial piety and affection to so high a place. But, following this, comes the other lesson of His transcendent superiority to her and to all His earthly relationships, and the unmistakable protest which He leaves by this incident against any undue exaltation of even His holy mother unto a place of peculiar veneration and worship. Therefore He calls her "woman" instead of mother, and transfers her, not to some place of deification, but to the humble protection of John and to the relationship of a mother to him. Therefore, if Mary has been lifted into a place of divinity, what place shall we give to John, her son?

The third lesson of this scene is the duty we owe to friends of Christ and the spiritual relationships into which we come to them through our union with Him so that they are to us truly as Mary was to John, as mother, and brothers and sisters. Here we see the dream of the household of faith and the family of God in its mutual as well as its divine relations, and the bonds of affection and care which are far too weak in the Church of God.

## 8. MARY MAGDALENE

Mary at the sepulchre, or the new revelation of the risen Lord (20:1-18).

This woman was singularly honored by the love of her risen Lord as the first witness of His resurrection. She had been saved from more than perhaps any of His disciples. His strong arm of love had rescued her from the sevenfold possession of demoniacal power. There is no reason to suppose that her womanhood had been degraded by the sin which has been associated with her name, but something more terrific, and on her part involuntary and irresistible, had bound perhaps all the powers of her body and soul. Set free by His almighty love, her heart was now bound to Him by cords of everlasting love.

No sadder or truer heart lingered at the cross through the dark hours of His dying agony, and no more fearless or devoted feet hastened on the Easter morning to anoint His body in Joseph's sepulchre. Finding the stone rolled away and the door open, she hastens to tell His brethren, Peter and John. When they have come and gone, she lingers still in the garden, believing that the body has been removed by the gardener's hands, perhaps, because of its being inconvenient to keep it longer. It is then that Jesus appears to her, disguised at first in a form that she mistakes for the gardener; but the disguise only brings out more beautifully her tender love. Her willing hands are ready to bear away the precious body, but His living voice dispels the illusion, and her hands clasp with rapture the feet of her Lord.

*HIS NEW RESURRECTION LIFE*

Dear as was her love to Jesus, and tenderly as He welcomed and responded to it, yet He saw that there was too much of the old human apprehension in her faith. She must be gently taught now to rise to the higher realization of His resurrection and His ascension life. Therefore He adds, "Touch me not" (20:17). It was as if He had said, "Think of Me henceforth as ascended to My Father and your Father, and go and tell My brethren." This was the same thought expressed by the apostle, namely, that though he had known the Lord Jesus after the flesh, yet now henceforth He knew Him thus no more.

Thus the cords that bound Mary's heart to Him were transformed from earth to heaven and her spirit taught to recognize Him as a spiritual presence while His body was to be enthroned at the right hand of God. Perhaps she had also to be taught to lose her own self-consciousness and joy in the thought of her brethren and the higher ministry of service. Henceforth her hands were not so much to clasp her Lord for her own exclusive possession, as to give Him forth for the salvation and consolation of others. Among the many sweet lessons of this beautiful incident we may learn:

a. Love is the element of highest vision. Mary's affection for her Lord led to her being the first to see Him.

b. Jesus is often with us unrecognized, even as Mary supposed Him to be the gardener.

c. Christ's love to us is personal. He called her by her own name, and then there was no mistake about His identity. They who know Him personally know Him unmistakably.

d. We must know Jesus spiritually, not by the touch of flesh, but by the contact of faith as the living and ascended One at God's right hand and yet the ever-present in our hearts and lives.

e. We must be unselfish in our love to Christ and remember that every revelation and blessing He bestows upon us is a trust for others, and must not be held as a selfish joy.

## 9. THOMAS

Thomas, or Christ's patience with our doubts (20:24-28).

a. Many of our doubts arise from neglected duty. Had Thomas been in his place on the first Sabbath evening, he would have been saved a week of agony. Were we always where Christ came to meet us, or bids us go, we should escape many conflicts. Much of our spiritual darkness comes from disobedience.

b. Much of Thomas' unbelief arose from self-will. He had ample evidence in the testimony of his brethren, but he had made up his mind that he must have his own way and his own kind of proof, and nothing else would satisfy him. So many persons have a preconceived plan of blessing or salvation, and their own will is the hindrance to the blessing they seek.

c. Much of Thomas' doubt arose from his deep love to Christ and his fear lest it might not be true. Many true-hearted Christians are chronic doubters. Their very love to the cross of Christ and the interests committed to them keep them in constant unrest as they bear their own burdens and anxieties. Christ has much sympathy for the doubts and fears He sees in the true-hearted, and while He chides and reproves them, yet He gently bears with these troubled ones and constantly proves to them how useless are their fears.

d. Christ sometimes meets our unreasonable and willful demands, but when He does, as in the case of Thomas, He makes us ashamed of our willfulness and shows us how little we needed the thing we so insisted upon. When Thomas was allowed to thrust his hand into his Saviour's side, he did not want to do it, and, no doubt, was thoroughly ashamed that he had ever asked it. The patience of Jesus in stooping to our unreasonableness may well break our hearts with love.

e. Thomas sets a good example to other doubters in putting himself in the way of getting light by assembling the next time with the disciples. And so, if the doubter would only come into the light, or even come to meet it, he would soon find, like Thomas, his Lord ready to shed the light of life on all his darkness.

f. Thomas was convinced, not by material evidence, but by the spiritual character of his Lord, by the heart-searching omniscience which read his own secret thoughts and by the tender grace and love which dealt so generously with his unbelief. And so we shall find the best answer to all our questionings in the manifestation of Jesus Himself to our hearts, as the Searcher of all their secrets and the Supply of all their needs.

g. Let us not miss the blessing here pronounced on the higher kind of faith which we all may have, and for which all the discipline of life is the best school, the faith of him who hath not seen and yet hath believed.

## 10. PETER

Peter's restoration, or Christ's love and grace for the backslider (21:15-22).

Already Peter had met the Lord alone and, doubtless, poured out his penitential confession at His feet and received, we may be sure, the Master's forgiveness; but weeks have elapsed since their return to Galilee, the Master had not come as He appointed and Peter's faith has begun to fail. This is doubtless the reason why he returned to his fishing nets and led with him, as his strong nature usually did, so many of his brethren. But their labor was all in vain, as it ever is when God is calling us from a forbidden path to Him.

On the incidents of the miracle that followed we do not dwell here, with all its significant teachings regarding their future service. Perhaps their thoughts had already reverted to that first miracle of the draught of fishes, where they had been called to become fishers of men. Peter may have been already wondering about the significance of this second call as they sat together at their morning meal on the shore. Then the words of Jesus fell upon his ear, "Simon, son of Jonas" (21:15). It was a good while since he had been called by that name, and it may have reminded him of his human weakness. There could be no question now of his Lord's meaning as he follows the name with the humiliating question, "Lovest thou me?" (21:15) especially as the word He uses is not the strongest word for love and seems to imply a doubt of the disciple's devotion. There is also a little hint in the words, "more than these" (21:15) reminding him of his claims of superior devotion the night on which He was betrayed. And in the threefold question as it is at length repeated, there is an unmistakable allusion to the threefold denial on that dreadful night. But Peter appeals to his Lord's omniscience, and using a far intenser word than Christ had used for love, he answers, "Yea, Lord; Thou knowest that I love Thee dearly" (21:15, author's paraphrase). He employs the strongest expression which language affords for the intensity of his love. The Lord accepts the answer and then gives him the first apostolic charge, "Feed my lambs" (21:15).

A second time He asks the question in the very same words, still using the colder term for love, and a second time Peter answers with the tenderer profession. The Lord adds the second apostolic charge, "Shepherd My sheep" (21:16, author's paraphrase).

The third time Jesus asks the question, using now at length the intense word for love which Peter had employed. Peter, grieved that he had again been doubted, appeals most solemnly to Christ's all-searching wisdom, and repeats his former asseveration, "Lord, Thou knowest all things, Thou knowest that I love Thee dearly" (21:17, author's paraphrase). Then Jesus gives the third apostolic command and the tenderest of all, "Feed My feeble sheep" (21:17, author's paraphrase), giving him that special ministry of consolation to the weak and tired which we find so exquisitely fulfilled in Peter's Epistle of consolation.

One lesson more is to be learned. It is the lesson of self-crucifixion—the surrender and subjugation of Peter's strong self-will and the suppression of his strong hand and curious inquiring mind with respect to others, even to John, his truest friend. "Another shall gird thee, and carry thee whither thou wouldest not"(21:18) is the message which sends him forth henceforth with bowed spirit and head to follow his Lord to the very cross itself. The other message with respect to John, "What is that to thee?

follow thou me" (21:22), silences all his questionings, takes his eyes off all but Jesus and lays at last all that is left of Simon, son of Jonas, in the bottomless sepulchre of his risen Lord.

# CHAPTER 8

# *TEN MIRACLES IN THE GOSPEL OF JOHN*

WE find ten remarkable miracles in John which are "signs" as well as wonders.

## *1. THE FIRST MIRACLE*

The Marriage at Cana (2:1-11).

This miracle was especially, as indeed all Christ's miracles were, a sign as well as a wonder, setting forth many underlying spiritual truths. This sign was especially significant of the whole teaching of John's Gospel, expressed in a single sentence; its chief lesson is the failure of the life of nature and the deeper and fuller life which Jesus brings us in the new creation.

The feast and wine of Cana represent earth's highest felicity, and the failure of Cana's wine expresses the blight which has fallen on all our human life and happiness. The new wine which Jesus brings is the figure of that divine life which He has come to impart to our lost humanity. All He needs is that the earthly vessel of our being shall be empty and then filled with the living water of His Holy Spirit and that we shall begin to pour it out in love and service. We find that it has become new wine, making all life a marriage feast and a foretaste of the marriage supper of the Lamb.

He that would enter into this blessed life must not forget the charge of Mary and the servants at Cana, "Whatsoever he saith unto you, do it." As we follow His word in faith and obedience, we shall find, as they did, that all our wants are supplied at His bidding and our life's deepest extremities transformed into occasions of overflowing blessing.

There is also in the marriage scene an obvious hint of that divine relationship with Himself, into which Jesus has come to bring us as the bridegroom of His church and the satisfaction of the deepest affections of the consecrated heart. Back of this picture there shines, in living characters, not only the glorious word *Life*, but the still loftier name of Love. There is also a delightful suggestion of the sympathy of Jesus with all human life in its innocent joys and the pure affections and pleasures of that sweet sanctuary which His own example has ever hallowed, the home.

## 2. THE TEMPLE CLEANSED

The Cleansing of the Temple (2:13-22).

Among the deeper teachings of this impressive miracle may be mentioned:

a. The authority of Jesus over the institutions of Judaism and the sanctuary of His Father's worship. This act was a bold assumption of His Messiahship.

b. The typical meaning of the temple as the symbol of His own body, and especially His mystical body, the Church, gives a deeper spiritual importance to His act of authority and judgment. He refers in the passage to this typical significance and speaks of His own body as the true temple which was to be destroyed and raised up again.

The conception of the Christian Church as the body and also as the temple of Christ is common to the New Testament Epistles. In this aspect the miracle emphasizes the necessity of the purity of the Church and her separation from the world, especially all worldly methods for her support. It would not be hard to find in a majority of the churches of today many a counterpart of the oxen, the sheep, the doves and the money-brokers of the ancient temple. We see it in the spirit of worldly conformity in the lives of many Christians; in the unhallowed entertainments which so often defile the sanctuary of God, covered by the flimsy excuse of the need of helping out the finances of the church; in the hired worldings that so often lead the service of praise with the flavor of the opera, the associations of the beer garden concert; and alas, in the mercenary spirit that too often controls the very ministry itself and reproaches the name of the Master.

The scourge of small cords which the Master used might explain many of the petty trials, afflictions, disappointments and failures of many a church which does not understand the chastening of its God and the lessons of its barrenness and failure.

c. The miracle, however, has a more personal application to the individual heart. If the Lord would come into this individual temple, it, too, must be cleansed, but He Himself is the only true Deliverer. Sometimes the first stage of His work is one of keen pain and sharp chastisement. As the first miracle teaches us the lesson of the new life, the second emphasizes the necessity of purity as the result of love and the very element of all Christ's blessings and teachings.

## 3. FAITH WITHOUT SIGHT

The Nobleman's Son (4:46-54).

The emphatic lesson of this miracle is, as we have already shown, the necessity of faith as the condition of Christ's work and blessing, especially the faith that rises above the visible and rests on His simple word. This also becomes a sign of the special teaching of John. It is an object lesson, in the beginning of the Gospel, of the principle which He declares in words at the end: "Blessed are they that hath not seen, and yet have believed" (20:29).

Over more than twenty miles of intervening space we see the instant working of Christ's mighty word and this man's immediate faith. With explicit detail it is added that the fever abated the very hour the man believed.

We see here, also, two stages of faith: faith, in the first instance, before he saw the result (4:50), and faith afterwards, in its fuller developments, when he and his household witnessed the consummation of the miracle (4:53). The first was a belief in Christ's word of healing. The second was a complete committal of his heart to Christ Himself in His character and teachings, and a deep and settled confidence arising from his deeper knowledge of Christ. This is what the apostle Paul expresses when he says, "I know whom I have believed" (2 Timothy 1:12).

## 4. THE GREAT PHYSICIAN

The Impotent Man at Bethesda (John 5:1-14).

The emphatic teaching of this miracle is the restoring ministry of Jesus in contrast with all man's superstitions and human attempts to help himself. The pool of Bethesda, with all its supposed virtues, is a fair specimen of man's various methods of help and healing both for soul and body. The very corruptions of the passage are an amusing hint of the foolish superstitions that human religions and remedies have heaped up through the centuries. The wretched failure of all for nearly half a century to help this poor sufferer is a fair commentary on the value of man's best attempts to save himself. It is scarcely necessary to explain that the words of verse 4 about the angel troubling the waters are an interpolation and do not belong to the text.

The sufferer, too, is an excellent illustration both of the physical and spiritual condition of most sinners. His greatest need is strength; his chief symptom, impotence both of muscle and of will. In healing him the Lord pays no regard to the pool of Beth-esda or his feeble complaints about getting somebody to help him when the waters are troubled, but simply asks him if he has will enough, or will exercise sufficient desire, to choose to be whole.

### FAITH AN ACT OF WILL

The Lord here teaches us that both in spiritual and physical healing the secret of faith is a decisive act of will. The moment we are ready to commit ourselves to God, definitely and irrevocably, He is willing to carry us through. Therefore, Christ requires of this man an instantaneous and decisive act of faith. "Rise, take up thy bed, and walk" (5:8). And the moment he obeys, the power already communicated to his will passes into his entire being, and the victim of nearly 40 years is well.

This miracle led to an important discussion about the limitations of the Sabbath which we shall elsewhere refer to. We have already seen that the fact of Christ's so often healing on the Sabbath was directly designed to rebuke the prevailing idea that sickness was a purely secular thing and the physician's art a matter of worldly business. Jesus ever taught that the body was as sacred as the soul, and divine healing as much a part of His sacred ministry as salvation.

Another hint is given in this miracle of the spiritual cause of his diseases. This was not always the case, but in the present instance it is certain that the long and weary sufferings of this man's life were the direct results of his own personal sin and that the continuance of his healing would depend upon a life of purity and obedience, while the neglect of this would bring him still more aggravated judgments.

## 5. THE MULTITUDE FED

The Feeding of the Five Thousand (John 6:5-14).

We notice in this miracle a beautiful progress in the spiritual truths unfolded by these signs.

The last miracle revealed Jesus as the Restorer of life, this as the sustainer and support of both our spiritual and physical life— the Living Bread by whom our entire being must be supplied with vital strength from day to day. The bread distributed to these multitudes did not cease with the setting sun on those Galilean hills, but still through all the ages since His ascension, it has been repeated, not always to the multitudes, but to every single heart that will come to Him and feed upon Him.

Some of the details which John gives us of this miracle are richly instructive. Two of the disciples are introduced in the preliminary conversation, and their perplexity and unbelief stands out in striking contrast with His own calm faith and power. Philip, like many of us, sees only the vastness of the multitude; Andrew, only the smallness of the resources, the five loaves and two small fishes. But Jesus calmly commands them to go forward and make all the arrangements for the feast. When the few loaves and fishes have been brought to Him, He blesses them and distributes them through the disciples. As they hand them to the people, one by one, lo, the bread is multiplied until all are satisfied, and the fragments that remain are enough to fill to overflowing the baskets of all the disciples.

We have here, therefore, not only a sign of the Living Bread, which we ourselves can feed upon, but of our responsibility to give it to the world and of the sufficiency of the feeble resources we may possess for our work. If we only bring them to Him and go forth with His blessing in the simple steps of faith and obedience, not only will we have enough for the world's need, however wide the world of our work may be, but when the work is done, our own baskets shall be overflowing and our own souls shall have been blessed, replenished and strengthened an hundredfold.

## 6. THE TEMPEST STILLED

The Stilling of the Tempest (6:16-21).

This is a revelation of Christ as He meets the next need of our human life. In our trials and dangers Christ is the Deliverer and Comforter.

First, He lets trial come to them, nay, often sends them forth before Him alone in the midst of the storm and the darkness of the night. So He sent His little Church out into the future without His visible presence, knowing the tempests of persecution and opposition that were to assail her through the long night of the dark ages. So also He sends forth each of us upon the path of life, through waves and clouds and storms; but we need not fear if He has sent us.

Secondly, He sees us from the mountaintop, and, indeed, is praying for us there amid all the tempests' rage; nor will He suffer the trial to become too great but will come in the right moment.

Thirdly, His coming to us as a spiritual presence, both in the Church's history and in the individual heart, is often misunderstood and unperceived. We are even afraid of the form of our Lord as unbelief distorts it, and even changes it, until it is a structure of terror. But we may always know Him by His voice, "It is I; be not afraid" (6:20). The true remedy for all our trials is just this personal Christ. He does not say it is morning, or it is calm weather, but "It is I." Not in circumstances, nor in ourselves, but in His blessed presence is our security and consolation.

Fourthly, but there is something better still, He is coming in person, perhaps on the tempest and billows of the wildest storm that the Church has ever known; but when He comes, it will be true again, "immediately the ship was at the land whither they went" (6:21). Her trials will be past, and long deferred hopes shall be realized. She shall be where tempests cease and surges swell no more.

## 7. THE BLIND MAN HEALED

The Blind Man at Jerusalem (9:1-38).

This is also a progressive unfolding of Jesus, now as the Light of the World; and not only the Light, but the giver of sight as well as external light and the Quickener of all our powers of spiritual vision if we are but willing to acknowledge our blindness and receive Him as our Teacher. Many definite lessons are taught us by this remarkable case of healing.

a. We learn that disease is not always caused by sin but is sometimes permitted in order that the power of God to heal may be more signally displayed. This man's blindness was not the result of special sin, either on his own part or his parents', but that the works of God might be made manifest in him, that is, of course, in his healing. What a blessing it would be if we would ever feel that our troubles have been permitted, not that we should sink under them, but that God might have an adequate occasion to show what He can do in our deliverance.

b. He definitely implies that his blindness was not the work of God but of another hand. The works of God were to be manifested in his healing. Not only was this Christ's work, but the Father's work which He had come to do; and so He seems to imply that when He shall have gone, night will again begin to fall upon the world. The works of the Father, in healing and restoring wrecked humanity, will in some measure cease—not through lack of the Father's will but rather of a willing instrument (9:4-5).

c. The method of this man's healing was through a double sign; first, the anointing of his eyes with clay, and second, the washing away of the clay in the pool of Siloam. Did Christ mean by this double sign to intimate the cause and the cure of our spiritual blindness; clay implying the touch of earth which has dimmed our vision, and then the pool, significant of the sent One, representing the washing from on high by which earth's clay is put away and our eyes are opened to the heavenly vision?

### NOT A REMEDY

To say that this application was the use of a remedy for his blindness and was a recognition of human remedies seems too absurd to need answer. If the clay was the remedy, it seems strange that he was not healed until it was washed away. If the pool was the remedy, why should it not be as efficacious in other cases? This was a case where no remedy could avail, for he was a man born blind, and remedy means something adapted to produce a result. Now nothing could be adapted in this case to produce the result, because it was impossible; therefore these two acts were but symbols of the divine touch and of the deeper spiritual lessons unfolded. As today, the anointing of oil in the name of the Lord is not a means of cure, but it is a visible sign of the divine touch upon the suffering one.

d. The testimony of this man is full of manly courage and keen discernment. He faces the whole synagogue and stands fearlessly for his Deliverer, amazed that anybody could doubt that One to whom God could give such power was a true teacher and divine messenger. Like many still who are not afraid to witness for all that God has done for them, his persecution ended in his being expelled from the synagogue. But like every similar trial, it brought him a greater blessing, for then the Master met him and led him into a deeper revelation of His own character and love. Prostrate at Jesus' feet his spiritual vision was now open and he recognized and worshiped the Son of God as his own Saviour and Lord. It teaches us that as we are true to Christ and to the light and blessing He gives us, He will lead us on and more freely meet us in every trial and suffering with the higher revelation of Himself.

## 8. HIS SUPREME MIRACLE

The Resurrection of Lazarus (11:1-45).

This completes the progress of development in this series of Christ's miracles, unfolding the last and highest stage of His work of grace and power, not only as the Restorer, Comforter, Sustainer and Healer of His people, but as the Conqueror of death and the Author of resurrection life. No other miracle of resurrection can be compared to this. Here corruption had already begun its work, and only Omnipotence could ever call back the spirit now four days in the world of the unseen. There was no possible cavil against this miracle. The Pharisees were silenced before its majesty and felt that their only resource was violence and murder.

It is not necessary to repeat here what has been said elsewhere upon this passage further than to call attention to the faith which He sought to awaken in Martha's mind, and which, there can scarcely be a doubt, He saw in Mary's simpler heart, but, above all, to the sublime faith of the Lord Himself. No mightier prayer has ever been uttered than this, "Father, I thank thee that thou hast heard me" (11:41). It is the pattern of victorious faith in the hour of all our trials, in the face of every dark disaster and consuming sorrow. It will open the gates of brass, and break in pieces the doors of iron and bring to us every deliverance consistent with the will of God and the possibilities of faith.

It was also the foreshadowing of the future resurrection. His words to Martha seem to include two classes who shall take part in the stupendous change which shall occur at His coming. First, there will be those who, like Lazarus, have long been sleeping in their graves, of whom it shall be true, "He that was dead shall live" (11:25, author's paraphrase). But secondly, there shall be those who shall be still alive at His appearing, and of them the next sentence shall be also true, "Whosoever that liveth and believeth in me shall never die" (11:26). Thus also does this miracle become a sign of spiritual truth, foreshadowing the resurrection and containing the pledge and guarantee of every victory and blessing we need to claim from Him who is still for each one of us as we will receive Him and trust Him, the Resurrection and the Life.

## 9. HIS VOLUNTARY SURRENDER

The Prostration of the Officers Who Came to Arrest Him (18:4-12).

There is no doubt that this manifestation of Christ's power was miraculous and was designed to impress these men with His ability to resist their force if He so desired and with the perfect voluntariness of His surrender and submission to their hands. Perhaps, also, it was designed to give weight to His demand that His own disciples should be exempted from arrest. "If therefore ye seek me, let these go their way" (18:8) is the condition on which He yields Himself to their power.

This incident gives a sublime meaning to all the events that immediately followed, culminating with His death. It makes His crucifixion an act of perfect self-sacrifice and invests the cross with all the grandeur of infinite love. Indeed, this is the view which predominates in John's picture of the last sufferings and death of Christ. The darker shadows are all omitted from the picture, and the cross is represented, not as His defeat and humiliation, but as the hour when the Son of Man was glorified. Therefore, the garden scene of conflict and agony is omitted and we behold Him rather as the Master of the situation, dictating His own terms to the very officers who stand before Him. So again, in the presence of the Sanhedrin, He stands in holy majesty, challenging a single word of testimony against Him. So, in Pilate's judgment hall He is the real judge, and Pilate himself the witness for His innocence. So, even on the cross the pall of darkness is omitted and the parting word is a shout of victory.

## 10. THE LAST MIRACLE

The Second Draught of Fishes (21:1-10).

This is the last sign recorded in this Gospel. Its significance is connected with the great theme of service for Christ to which the apostles were now to be called in a higher and mightier sense than during His earthly ministry.

a. There is an undoubted allusion to the former draught of fishes three years before and its significance of their first call to apostolic service. This would naturally be associated with a similar call, although, of course, in a higher sense.

b. There is a suggestion in the background of the miracle of their having, in some measure, gone back from their high calling and begun at last to falter in their faith and courage. And so the lesson is, in some sense, a message to the Master's discouraged and unfaithful disciples—those who, doubting their Master's faithfulness, have gone back to some old place of worldly compromise or earthly occupation from which He had previously separated them. In such a place it is a great mercy if, like the seven disciples, we too have a wretched time and find all our efforts unavailing and lost.

c. The appearance of Jesus on the shore in the gray dawn was unrecognized; and the disciple who is out of his Lord's will, will be very likely to miss even the vision of his Lord through the blinding influence of unbelief and worldly occupation.

d. The command of Christ to cast the net on the other side, and the immediate results in the miraculous draught of fishes, reveal the Master. John is the first to recognize Him because his spirit was the least clouded by unbelief, and Peter is the first to plunge for the shore. The other disciples followed in a little fishing boat, dragging the loaded net and landing it, with Peter's help, with its enormous store of great fishes, every one of which is safely landed and the net unbroken. All this is so different from the former miracle, where the net broke and the ship began to sink, and Peter, in guilty awe, begged the Master to depart from him because he felt unworthy of His presence, that it must itself have suggested to their minds the higher lessons it has taught the church of service for Christ and the Church.

e. The chief of these lessons is the higher service upon which they were now to enter into fellowship with their risen Lord, and of which Peter, who had just dragged the net to land, was to be the first illustrious example through his harvest of souls on the day of Pentecost. They were to learn the vanity and unselfishness of all their wisdom and strength in the Master's work, and the necessity of His presence and guidance as they cast the gospel net into the sea of sinful men. Only as He stood upon the shore were they able to cast it upon the right side, and only as they spake and acted in fellowship with Him would they be able to bring to land the souls they sought to save. But henceforth that presence and power was to be their resource.

Henceforth, the imperfect work which had ended in their desertion and denial of the Lord was to be repeated no more. Abiding in Him they should bring forth much fruit and their fruit should remain. Their fishes should be brought to land, and in the great day should be all counted upon the heavenly shore, like the great fishes on the Galilean morning, the glorious and eternal memorials of their work.

Not only so, but their morning meal upon the beach, upon the very fishes which they had caught, was intended to teach them that their work should be their future reward. In a very blessed sense they should feed upon its fruits, both now and in the eternal morning. In a little while, for every true worker, the vision will be fulfilled. The last long night of sorrow will be over, and the golden shore will be just ahead with His blessed Face and His beckoning Hand calling us to His presence. One last plunge like Peter's into the dark waters, and we shall be there; the last wave shall be passed, the last shadow gone. As He seats us at His table and says to us, "Come and dine," we shall know it is the Lord. We shall recognize among the richest joys and recompenses of the eternal banquet the tears we have dried on earth, the sins we have covered with His blood, the steps we have recalled from the paths of sin, the souls we have warned from death, the lives we have given to His love and the blessed ones we shall find awaiting us in His presence and hailing us as the instruments of their eternal happiness.

# CHAPTER 9

## *CHRIST'S DISCOURSES IN THE GOSPEL OF JOHN PART 1*

THE Gospel of John contains several discourses of the Lord Jesus. Some of them were addressed to individuals, some of them were public addresses in the temple and the last two were parting discourses to His immediate disciples at the table and on the way to the garden. Let us first notice two of His personal discourses, the first with Nicodemus, the second with the woman of Samaria.

### 1. THE NEW BIRTH AND THE NEW LIFE (John 3).

a. The necessity of the new birth and the new life.

It is more than knowledge, and it is essential to all true spiritual knowledge. Nicodemus can say "We know," but Jesus replies, "Except a man be born again, he cannot see the kingdom of God" (3:3). The very first glimpse of spiritual truth is impossible without the new birth. Nicodemus was, undoubtedly, a man of superior morality, but morality without spiritual life can no more lift the soul into the kingdom of God than nature and pruning can change a bramble into a man, or even into an apple tree.

A poor Negro in the South once brought the two hands of a clock to a watchmaker to be repaired, complaining that they would not keep time. The watchmaker laughed at his ignorance and told him to go home and bring the clock, or, at least, the works of the clock. The Negro explained that the clock was all right, the trouble was all in the hands. They would not keep proper time. He went away complaining that the tradesman wanted to draw him into an unnecessary bill for the repairing of the clock and trying to find some other workman that would repair his irregular clock-hands.

A good many people are like the poor African, trying to repair the hands of their poor broken down human nature, not knowing or thinking that the fatal ruin is in the deeper springs of the heart and that what they need is not reformation, but regeneration.

b. The nature of regeneration.

It is described as a new birth. Elsewhere it is called a new creation. It is the addition of a new element in human nature, namely, spiritual life; spoken of in the latter Scriptures as nothing less than a new man. It is not the creation of new intellectual faculties or physical powers, but a new spiritual principle. Here it is contrasted with John's baptism, "born of water," This is more, being born from above and of the Spirit. Again, it is contrasted with being born of the flesh. This term, *flesh*, includes not only the physical, but also the psychical nature.

It is not always possible to perceive the processes, any more than it is to follow the viewless wind, but we may know the reality and power of both by their effects.

Regeneration is not complete sanctification. It is the birth not of an Adam, full grown, but of a feeble infant. But it will mature into all the fullness of the stature of a man in Christ. It is real and complete in all its parts, in its infancy as in its manhood, just as the babe is as perfectly human as its grandfather, though not as old or as fully developed.

c. The Author of the new birth is the Holy Spirit (3:5, 8).

He is the source of all life, and His highest work is to bring souls into the life of God. The regeneration of the soul is as divine a result as the creation of a world and involves the putting forth of a mightier effort of omnipotence.

d. The new birth is brought about through the gospel of the Lord Jesus Christ.

Therefore, the Lord Jesus adds the beautiful words from the thirteenth to the eighteenth verses respecting His coming and the necessity of faith in Him.

The new life is received by believing in the Son of God, even as the wounded Israelites received life and healing by looking at the uplifted serpent of brass in the midst of the camp. The ancient symbol vividly expresses both sides of the process of salvation. The uplifted serpent prefigured the crucified Saviour, held up as the object of our faith. The steadfast gaze upon it finely expresses the look of faith toward Jesus, by which the soul receives His imparted life.

And in the closing sentences the Lord refers to the instrumentality of the truth in the great work of regeneration. The new creation, like the old, begins with the coming in of light (3:19). They who receive the light are soon led into the life of God, but they who hate and reject the light receive a double condemnation simply on the ground of its rejections. "This is the condemnation, that light is come into the world, and men loved darkness rather than light, because their deeds were evil" (3:19).

## 2. SPIRITUAL LIFE, WORSHIP AND SERVICE (4:10-38).

### a. Spiritual life.

The Lord sets forth the blessedness of the life which He has come to bring into our hearts by the figure of the water of Sychar. Like all of her race, this poor woman had been seeking for life from the broken cisterns of earthly pleasure, but Jesus reveals to her the deeper fountains of life which she may have from Him and henceforth carry in her very heart as a well of water in her, springing up into everlasting life.

### b. Spiritual worship.

He next leads her thoughts from her sectarian prejudices and her external ritualism to the higher principles of true religion which He had come to unfold—the fact that God was not confined to places or temples made with hands, but that His true temple is the spirit of man. The worship which He requires is the spiritual devotion of the heart, the conformity of the life to His word and truth, to the knowledge and love of Him in His divine Fatherhood.

"God is a Spirit: and they that worship him must worship him in spirit and in truth. . . . for the Father seeketh such to worship Him" (4:24 ,23).

c. Spiritual service (4:34-38).

These words were addressed to His own disciples after the woman left, but they contain the true sequel to the former discourse. From the figure of the natural harvest, now whitening upon the fields, He passes to the thought of the great spiritual harvest to which He was calling His disciples, and of which He had just given them an illustration in the salvation of this woman, and the still larger fruitage which was coming, even as He spake, in the thronging Samaritans whom she brought to Him.

He tells them that such service is the very meat and nourishment of His own soul and will bring to them, not only the partnership of His joy, but a glorious recompense besides, in the hour of His coming. There are wages now which the true worker receives from day to day, but there is a still more blessed partnership in the harvest itself, for "He that reapeth receiveth wages, and gathereth fruit unto life eternal" (4:36).

And then He refers to the indirect results of our work through the work of others, and especially of those that we have led to Christ as illustrated in the beautiful example of this woman who has not only been saved herself, but has now gone forth and multiplied the fruit in the salvation of hundreds of others. So He teaches them that their work shall thus involve the fellowship of others, and together they shall share the eternal recompense. "He that soweth and he that reapeth may rejoice together" (4:36).

One more lesson He adds in connection with this spiritual harvest, namely: the necessity of immediate and prompt action. We are always in danger of dreaming of the future, but in spiritual service opportunity is a passing angel and must be held by the hand of instant decision. "Say not ye, There are yet four months, and then cometh harvest? . . . Lift up your eyes, and look on the fields; for they are white already to harvest" (4:35). And as in the natural, so also in the spiritual husbandry; the fields will not wait our convenience or caprice, but the ripened grain will perish if it is not garnered. Every day brings its irrevocable opportunities, and if lost they, at least, will never return.

# CHAPTER 10

# CHRIST'S DISCOURSES
# IN THE GOSPEL OF JOHN
# PART 2

CONTINUING the discourses of our Lord in the Gospel of John we come to

## 3. CHRIST AND THE FATHER (5:17-38).

### a. His Deity.

In this passage Christ makes His first public claim in the presence of the Jews of equality with His Father and gives this as the reason for His healing the impotent man on the Sabbath. In doing this He was simply coworking with God, who, from the beginning of the creation, has exercised His active omnipotence every moment in sustaining the universe and giving life and strength to all beings. Christ was doing only the same thing in restoring strength to this man on the Sabbath day.

The Jews perfectly understood His meaning. Now, with a double ground of hostility against Him because He has insulted the Sabbath law, and His alleged blasphemy in claiming equality with God, they began seriously to plot His destruction.

Christ follows up His statement by declaring His absolute dependence upon the Father for all His works and at the same time His equal partnership in all the Father's works. He then announces that He is yet to manifest still mightier works in the Father's name which will fill them with astonishment. Two of these He specifies; namely, the quickening of the dead and the prerogative of judgment upon every human soul. The purpose of all this He declares to be the Father's glory, "That all men should honour the Son, even as they honour the Father" (5:23).

b. The Son's message and gift of love and salvation to men in His Father's name.

Invested with this high authority and power, He comes to men and now offers them, through faith in His word, the gift of everlasting life.

First, it is a present quickening through His living voice and almighty power. "The hour is coming, and now is, when the dead shall hear the voice of the Son of God: and they that hear shall live" (5:25). This, of course, refers to the spiritual life which Jesus now imparts to the soul dead in trespasses and sin. Second, it is a life that delivers from condemnation and judgment by the law, and which takes us out of the place of guilt altogether and gives us eternal acquittal and justification through the decree of the very One who is Himself the Judge (5:24-27). Third, it unfolds the future resurrection of the body (5:29). This, then, is Christ's great message and gift to men in His Father's name: life spiritually, life judicially and life immortal in the resurrection.

c. The credentials of this divine message (5:30-39).

What evidence does He bring to prove His high authority and the truth of His wonderful message? He does not ask them to receive Him on His own mere word, but He brings four great credentials:

The witness of John which they have already accepted in other respects.

The witness of His Father which has been explicitly given in His behalf.

The witness of His own works as proof of His divinity.

The very Scriptures on which they founded all their institutions and hopes bear unequivocal testimony to Him who is the fulfillment of all prophecy and the end of all the teachings of even Moses in whom they trust (5:46-47)—credentials they cannot and do not attempt to dispute.

d. Their rejection of Him and the message of love He brings.

In the face of all this evidence they willfully refused to receive Him. "Ye will not come to me, that ye might have life" (5:40). Or it might be made even more emphatic, "Ye will not to come." It is a perverse obstinacy in spite of truth and evidence.

The reason of their unbelief He also tells them. First, it is because they have not the love of God in them; their heart is not single unto Him. Where this is the case there can never be the true light of faith. Secondly, they are under the influence of human opinions and selfish aims. "How can ye believe which receive honor from one another, and not that which cometh from God only?" (5:44, author's paraphrase).

What a solemn intimation of the danger of a divided heart in perverting the soul and blinding it even to the light of life. And yet, He warns them as He closes that, although so unwilling to believe Him with all the light and evidence He brings, they will become the willing dupes of a thousand impostors and perhaps, at last, of the very Antichrist who will deceive them as the counterfeit of the true Messiah.

### 4. CHRIST, THE LIVING BREAD (CHAPTER 6).

This address, as we have already seen, was given in Galilee at the close of His ministry there and immediately after the feeding of the five thousand—perhaps on the Sabbath of the Passover which was then being celebrated in Jerusalem. Its one great theme, the revelation of Jesus Christ in His person as the satisfaction of all the soul's needs, in contrast with their earthly expectations of a Messiah who was to give them mere human bread and relieve them from their temporal burdens and disasters. They were eager to make Christ their king if He would always feed them with such bread as His great miracle had furnished, but when He came to lead them to a closer fellowship with Himself and to require a deeper and more spiritual apprehension of Him, they turned away and rejected Him altogether.

This discourse consists of seven sections, marked by the interruptions of His audience and rising in succession to the final climax when the crisis is reached and their decision is made.

a. The true bread, in contrast with the meat which perisheth (6:26-27).

"Labour not," He says, "for the meat which perisheth, but for that meat which endureth unto everlasting life, which the Son of Man shall give unto you: for He hath God the Father's stamp" (6:26, author's paraphrase). This latter expression seems to refer to the ancient habit of putting a stamp, or trademark, on bread to indicate that it was the genuine production of a responsible tradesman. Christ bears the stamp of heaven as the True Bread of the world. They are seeking rather that which satisfies their earthly appetites, and He desires to elevate their thoughts and desires to the true source of spiritual life.

  b. The true way to receive this bread (6:28-29).

"Labour not," He says to them, "for the meat which perisheth" (6:27). "What then," they ask, "shall we work? What are the works of God?" (6:28, author's paraphrase). And He answers, "This is the work of God, that ye believe on him whom He hath sent" (6:29). The one thing He requires of you is not that ye shall labor for His free salvation but that ye receive it with simple trust, by believing on Him whom He hath sent.

  c. The heavenly character of this Bread in contrast, even, with the manna of the desert (6:30-33).

They now appeal to their own history and the great miracle of Moses in giving them manna in the desert for forty years. They ask for some corresponding sign of His claims to the faith which He has demanded of them. In this request we see already the beginning of their perverse unbelief. Had He not already given them in the miracle in Galilee a sign as great as the miracle of Moses?

So He does not meet them on their own plane by contrasting the greatness of His power with that of Moses but seeks to raise their thoughts to a more spiritual plane. He tells them that even the bread which Moses gave them, with all its manifestation of power, was not from heaven but after all but mere earthly food. Even if He should give them such bread continually it would not be the real satisfaction they needed. Therefore, He brings them bread from heaven itself, even the life which man has lost and which only the divine love can restore.

  d. Simpler and fuller explanation of this spiritual bread (6:34-40).

For a moment they seem to grasp His meaning, and they respond, "Lord, evermore give us this bread" (6:34).

He tells them that this bread is nothing less than His own personal life imparted to them. It is all wrapped up in Himself. It is not "I give the bread," but "I am the Bread of Life," and to possess it there must be a personal relation to and fellowship with Him.

This is the source of the only true rest and satisfaction. "He that cometh to me shall never hunger; and he that believeth on me shall never thirst" (6:35).

This is available and welcome to all who will truly receive it. There is no barrier in the way of any willing heart, either on the part of His Father or Himself. For Himself, He is so willing to receive any seeking soul that He puts on record the most absolute and unconditional of all His promises, "Him that cometh to me I will in no wise cast out" (6:37).

This is an invitation which admits anybody and everybody who is desirous not only of the saving mercy, but also of the sanctifying, satisfying and all-sufficient grace of Jesus to the last moment of life. Nor is His Father less willing to welcome sinful men. His very purpose in sending the Son, and His very will for men, is that they should thus be saved and satisfied. And even if Christ were less willing than He is, He would yet be bound, by His Father's will, to save men (6:38-39).

This life and satisfaction shall be eternal, reaching down beyond the grave and including the resurrection of the body in the last day (6:40).

e. Opposition of the Jews to His teachings concerning His own person as their life; and reiterations by Christ of this especial truth, with an additional reference now not only to His life, but also to His death (6:41-51).

The opposition of the Jews was on account of His high pretensions in contrast with what they knew of His obscure human origin. "Is not this Jesus, son of Joseph, whose father and mother we know? how is it that He saith, I came down from heaven?" (6:42).

Jesus answers them that no one can understand His divine character without divine teaching. "No man can come to me, except the Father which hath sent draw him" (6:44). And this, He adds, lest they should excuse themselves by saying that the Father had not drawn them: "Every man therefore that hath heard, and hath learned of the Father, cometh unto me" (6:45). That is to say, the Father is teaching and willing to teach all who will learn; but they are not willing to be thus definitely taught and drawn.

Then He adds two new thoughts to His former teaching, respecting the life He brings to men. First, the life it brings is not like the nourishment imparted by the manna, mere mortal life, but it is everlasting life. "Your fathers did eat manna . . . and are dead" (6:49). "He that believeth on me hath everlasting life" (6:47). The other thought is that this life must come through His death; "The bread that I will give is my flesh, which I will give for the life of the world" (6:51).

f. This life must be received through vital union with the person of Christ and living communion with Him. More and more His hearers become perplexed with this idea of eating His flesh. He now adds to it the other expression, drinking His blood, these together expressing most perfectly the idea of an actual participation in His death and risen life. Like many since, they understood it literally and naturally asked, "How can this man give us his flesh to eat?" (6:52).

Jesus, however, now explains that what He means is such a union with Him as He has with the Father, by virtue of which His life is constantly sustained, not by natural means alone, but by the constant impartation of the divine life. "The living Father hath sent me, and I live by the Father: so he that eateth me, even he shall live by me" (6:57). And then He adds, to show how close the union thus involved is, "He that eateth my flesh, and drinketh my blood, dwelleth in me, and I in him" (6:56).

This was the constant support of His own physical and spiritual life, so that when tempted by the devil in the wilderness to make the stones into bread, He answered, "Man shall not live by bread alone, but by every word that proceedeth out of the mouth of God" (Matthew 4:4). This was not only for Himself, but is implied in the expression "man"—not the Son of Man only.

g. This can be fully understood and realized through the Holy Spirit's teaching and after His death, resurrection and ascension (John 6:60-65). Not in His present life among them, as they see Him with their eyes and touch Him with their hands, can He become to them fully the living bread. After He has ascended to His Father's right hand and sent forth the Holy Ghost to be the teacher and revealer of His truth and grace, and to lead His disciples to know and receive Him in His fullness, then shall these words be understood and appreciated.

"What," He says, "and if ye shall see the Son of Man ascend up where He was before? It is the Spirit that quickeneth; the flesh profiteth nothing: the words that I speak unto you, they are spirit and they are life" (6:62-63). Therefore Mary Magdalene, as she clasped His feet with her loving arms, must be taught that there was a higher touch and a more spiritual communion to which she must rise. "Touch Me not . . . but go to My brethren, and say unto them, I ascend unto My Father, and your Father, to My God, and your God" (20:17).

This was too spiritual for their carnal hearts, and so, we read, "many of His disciples went back, and walked no more with Him" (8:66). And this is the reason today that the multitudes of professing Christians know little of these great spiritual mysteries. They bring them too close to Christ and require too pure an element of living for their earthly tastes and aspirations.

## SUMMARY OF THE TEACHINGS OF THIS CHAPTER

(1) The earthly bread is the type of the higher needs and supplies of our being which Jesus comes to bring.

(2) Jesus Christ, in His own person, is the supply of all our needs. He is able and willing to impart His own very life as the strength and support of our entire being—spirit, soul and body. God has put into this one ideal Man all that man needs and needs to be, and He offers Himself to each one of us as the very substance of our life.

(3) This divine provision began with His death for us as our ransom. His flesh was given for the life of the world in the sense of substitution, first. This, therefore, is the primary meaning of drinking His blood, namely, partaking of the benefits of His death and atonement.

(4) But there is a far deeper meaning—not only His death, but His risen life, becomes for us the source of life. Not only did He give His life for us, but He also gives it to us. His blood repre-

sents His life, and His flesh represents, especially, His physical life. Both together express the fact that Jesus Christ, in His entire humanity, offers Himself to His people as their imparted life and strength; His holiness, love, joy, power and even His physical vitality to be the support and supply of our every spiritual and physical need.

(5) In order to receive Him thus, there must be a very intimate union with Him expressed by the language: "He that dwelleth in me, and I in him. (6:56). There must also be a habitual receiving of Him, expressed by the figure of eating and drinking, and also by the less figurative expression, "He that cometh to me . . . he that believeth on me" (6:35), etc.

(6) Not in His earthly, but in His ascension life, was this to be realized. Therefore, since Christ's resurrection He has been real to His people as He could not be before (6:62).

(7) We must be led into this knowledge of Christ and this best fellowship with Him by divine teaching. No man can thus come without the Father's drawing and the Spirit's revealing (6:44, 63, 65).

(8) But the Father is always teaching and the Spirit always drawing, and the Son always ready to receive all that come. Nowhere, in all His teachings, do we find such an assurance of the willingness of Christ to receive the soul that comes to Him as in the very midst of these present teachings. This is not the exclusive privilege of a favored class, but without limitation it is said of all who are willing to come, "Him that cometh to me I will in no wise cast out" (6:37). This is not only true of the soul that comes to Christ for salvation, but just as true of every advancing stage of our Christian life; and, especially, of this deeper experience into which the Lord is ever waiting and willing to lead His hungry and thirsty children.

(9) The climax of all this experience will be reached in the future resurrection. Therefore Christ adds repeatedly in this passage, "I will raise him up at the last day" (6:40, 44, 54). Then shall we know all that is involved in perfect union and fellowship with the person of our Lord as we share both in our body, our spirit and our future glory all the fullness of His life and all the riches of His glory.

# CHAPTER 11

# *CHRIST'S DISCOURSES IN THE GOSPEL OF JOHN PART 3*

THIS and the following discourse were delivered at the Feast of Tabernacles. The first, on the Living Water, consists of a number of broken paragraphs spoken successively during the feast and culminating in the striking address delivered on the last day of the feast (7:32-38). It might be divided into three sections:

## 5. THE LIVING WATER (John 7)

a. The condition of true spiritual knowledge (7:16-18).

This seems to be intended as an answer to their question respecting His wonderful wisdom in view of His obscure origin. He then tells them the true principle on which the divine knowledge depends, namely, a right spirit and an obedient heart. "If any man will do his will, he shall know of the doctrine" (7:17). He seems to imply that this is the reason why He Himself has been so divinely taught because His own aim and spirit are true to the Father's glory (7:18). But still more must this be true of all who hear Him. If they would understand His doctrine, which is not to be apprehended by the mere intellect, its true organ must be the heart and the will.

The word for *will* here is the strongest in the Greek language; literally, it means, "If any man *will to do His will*, He shall know the doctrine." The things of God, especially the deeper truths of Christianity, must become living experiences. God loves us too

well to give us more light than we will really follow for it would
but add the greater condemnation.

b. Jesus next proceeds to vindicate His own conduct in healing the impotent man on the Sabbath by citing the case of cir-
cumcision, which they frequently administered on the Sabbath,
and yet were held blameless, while He is accused of breach of the
law by healing a sufferer on this day (7:21-24).

c. He next bears witness again to His divine descent and His
heavenly origin. Still, His enemies listen with exasperation, but
so great is His hold upon the people that none of them dare to
touch Him. At length, however, the Pharisees are compelled to
make some show of boldness, and they send a band of officers to
arrest Him (7:32).

d. Jesus intimates in these words (7:33-34) that He will soon
be withdrawn from their midst and that many will seek Him in
vain, and, indeed, never find Him. Perhaps He refers to the
mournful days which were coming so soon to them when, beset
by their enemies and by the resistless legions of Rome, they
should look in vain for their Messiah. Perhaps some of them even
should remember how they had neglected and mocked His
blessed teachings, but they should see Him no more, "For
whither I go ye cannot come" (7:34, author's paraphrase).

e. His great discourse on the last day of the feast.

It is the final Sabbath of the Feast of Tabernacles. Processions
of priests are carrying the vessels of water from the pool of
Siloam and pouring it out on the sacred altar. Dense crowds fill
all the courts, and the interest of the whole festival is at its height.
Suddenly, in the midst of the celebration, Jesus lifts up His voice
and cries aloud in words which, no doubt, run through all the
corridors and courts, in the ears of thousands, "If any man thirst,
let him come unto Me, and drink. He that believeth on Me . . .
out of the midst of his being shall flow rivers of living water"
(7:37-38, author's paraphrase).

The allusion to the chief ceremony of the feast was so vivid
and the language so striking, while, no doubt, His manner added
unutterable weight to the entire scene, that the profoundest impression was made upon multitudes of the hearers. Even the officers who had come to take Him were overwhelmed with awe and

went away, not daring to touch Him.

The address itself leads us into spiritual truths as deep and precious as the preceding chapter. In that Jesus had not only alluded to the feeding of the five thousand, but also to two of the most ancient and venerable types of Judaism, namely, the Passover, which was being observed in Jerusalem, and the manna with which the people had been fed in the wilderness. In the present passage He alludes not only to the ceremony just being observed in the temple, but also to another of the most sacred of the Mosaic types, namely, the smitten rock of Horeb and the flowing water which had supplied the thirst of God's ancient people in the wilderness. Thus He dares to attribute to Himself two of the most significant of the types of their history by claiming to be at once the Bread and the Water of Life.

But, true to the spirit of the New Testament, He carries the figure farther than Judaism could. Here it is not merely received in selfish enjoyment and blessing, but it is given forth in still larger streams of beneficence to others. The same figure had been alluded to in His conversation with the woman of Samaria, but here it is much bolder and grander. There, the grace of Jesus was presented as the fountain in her own heart, but here it is the overflowing floods of many rivers pouring out their fullness in blessing to the world.

The evangelist himself has given us the interpretation, referring as it does to the Holy Spirit as He was to be poured out upon the disciples at Pentecost and to become henceforth the impulse of Christian life and the separation and power of consecrated service. He adds that the Holy Ghost was not yet given, or, literally, was not yet, because that Jesus was not yet glorified. It was necessary that the work of the Son should be finished on earth and He glorified at the Father's right hand before His divine Successor could come to administer the next stage of the kingdom of God. We may, therefore, believe that under the ancient dispensation and even during the life of Christ the Holy Ghost was not imparted to the people of God in His personal fullness as He has been since Christ's ascension.

There is a solemn personal lesson for every one of us in the expression here used; not only was it true dispensationally, but it must ever be true individually. The Holy Ghost will not be given until Jesus is fully glorified (see John 7:39). He comes still when Christ is fully exalted and all is laid at His feet; and He comes not to exalt us, or witness to us, but to glorify still Jesus only in our lives and services.

## 6. JESUS THE LIGHT OF THE WORLD (8:12; 9:39-41).

Another beautiful custom connected with the Feast of Tabernacles is referred to in this discourse, namely, the hanging of brilliant lamps in the Court of the Women. Pointing, perhaps, to these, Jesus exclaims, "I am the light of the world: He that followeth me shall not walk in darkness, but shall have the light of life" (8:12).

There may also have been an allusion to another Old Testament type, namely, the pillar of fire which led ancient Israel in the wilderness, thus connecting Christ with the whole system of Mosaic types, the manna in the wilderness, the rock in Horeb and the guiding presence of the cloud and Shekinah.

a. Christ is the Light of life; not merely a teacher of truth in the abstract, but a practical and personal guide. The light He gives is the light of life, that is, light that men can live by, shining on the path of duty, perplexity and trial, illuminating and cheering every step of Christian life. It can be enjoyed only by him who follows Christ. The essential condition is humble obedience. And the reason they could not understand it was because they were not willing to submit themselves to His will and direction.

b. It is divine light authorized by the witness of heaven and shed forth by One who has Himself come down from heaven and knows all worlds, all the possibilities of existence and all the secrets of time and eternity (8:14-19).

c. It is indispensable light, and without it they must perish in their sins (8:21-24).

d. It is light which they themselves shall yet recognize as true but too late to be of any avail for them. After they have rejected Him and wrecked themselves, they shall see their fatal error. Perhaps He intimates that some of them shall even then believe on Him (8:28).

e. It is light that leads to liberty and holiness (8:41-47).

They are the slaves of a master whom they are not willing to acknowledge and the subjects of a bondage more bitter than that of Egypt. "Whosoever committeth sin is the servant of sin" (8:34). They are bound by its fetters. Notwithstanding all their claims of descent from Abraham, they are not only the captives, but the very children of Satan. But He is the great Liberator as well as the light of the world. If they will believe the truth which He brings and enter into the Sonship which He offers to share with them, they will become free from the power of guilt and sin. They will rise to all the dignity of His own Sonship and all the privileges of the free-born children of God. Hence, the apostle Paul says to those who receive Him, "Wherefore thou art no more a servant, but a son. . . . God hath sent forth the Spirit of his Son in your hearts crying, Abba, Father" (Galatians 4:7, 6).

True spiritual freedom springs from the belief of the truth and personal union with the Son of God. To believe God's promises saves us from the consciousness of guilt and brings us into the power of full salvation. But this full salvation involves the indwelling presence and life of Christ Himself in our heart as the divine and overcoming power that breaks the bonds of evil. "The law of the Spirit of life in Christ Jesus hath made [us] free from the law of sin and death" (Romans 8:2).

A mere abstract faith, therefore, is not enough; there must be a living fellowship with Christ. Therefore, He says to the new converts who have accepted His word, "If ye continue in my word, then are ye My disciples indeed; and ye shall know the truth, and the truth shall make you free. If the Son therefore shall make you free, ye shall be free indeed" (John 8:31-32, 36).

Is there any soul under the bondage of guilt? The remedy is Christ's blessed word of redemption and forgiveness. "He that heareth My word, and believe on Him that sent Me, hath everlasting life, and shall not come into condemnation; but is passed from death unto life" (5:24).

Is there any soul under the power of sin? The same word waits to emancipate the soul, if it will but believe it and step forth upon it. "Now ye are clean through the word which I have spoken unto you" (15:3).

Is there any soul bound by physical evil and suffering? Only let it believe His gracious word that He has come to bear our sicknesses and carry our infirmities, and it has the strong and immovable resting place for a faith that can claim all needed strength and deliverance.

Is there any soul oppressed by Satan's temptations? All it needs is to know the truth that it is free and that Satan is a conquered foe. It needs to stand upon the glorious promises, "He hath spoiled principalities and powers" (Colossians 2:15, author's paraphrase); "Thou shalt tread upon the lion and adder" (Psalm 91:13); and lo! it steps out into victory and claims its full redemption rights.

During the American war some of the slaves were held by their former masters for many months after the Emancipation Proclamation had been issued. The poor captives were helpless and hopeless in their ignorance of their new freedom; but when the message reached them they knew the truth, and the truth made them free. And they arose at once to claim their lawful rights under the president's decree.

So the gospel is the divine proclamation of emancipation, and all men may claim it for themselves and enter into the fullness of their liberty. But not only have they the decree of liberty, but also the living power of the Son Himself, as the Captain of their salvation, to lead them into their freedom and conquer for them all the power that would resist their emancipation. Therefore, He adds, "If the Son therefore shall make you free, ye shall be free indeed" (John 8:36).

f. Light in the valley of the shadow of death (8:51-55).

Not only does this glorious light lead us forth from our captivity, as the pillar of cloud and fire led Israel out of Egypt, but it also goes down before us as the ark went through the Jordan into the valley and shadow of death.

"If a man keep my saying, he shall never see death" (8:51). This does not mean that the act and effect of mortality shall never touch his life, but that his spiritual consciousness shall be lifted above it. Though the body may sink and the eyes of our dearest friends may see what seems to be death, yet the triumphant spirit shall be carried above it so enwrapt with the presence of Christ and the consciousness of His enfolding life and indwelling joy that there shall be no real consciousness of death. The victorious spirit shall pass through without a shadow into the intenser, purer and more delightful joys of the heavenly world without a moment's interruption of its conscious life and perfect felicity. Has this not often been witnessed as the last experience of God's departing saints? Standing on the very brink of two worlds, they have whispered back to all around them, "There is no river here; it is light and joy." There was indeed no death.

g. The light of past ages and ancient saints and prophets (8:56).

"Your father Abraham rejoiced to see my day: and he saw it, and was glad" (8:56). This was the light that shone in the lamps of fire that passed through Abraham's vision on the night of sacrifice. This was the light which rose on the altar of Mt. Moriah when Isaac was given back to his arms from the funeral pile. This was the light that shone above the midnight stars in the promise of the everlasting covenant and the future Seed; the Light of Ages.

h. The light of spiritual vision (chapter 9).

The connection of this chapter is uncertain. The sense seems to link with the eighth chapter which we have just been considering, but many judicious interpreters consider it really a part of chapter ten and spoken at the Feast of Dedication a few months later. The passage (10:22), they think, points back to the whole preceding section and not merely to the verses that immediately follow. If this were so, there would be a double allusion in the figure of light still employed; not only to the healing of the blind man and the previous discourse about light, but also to the name often given to this feast as the Feast of Lights. One part of this imposing ceremony consisted of the suspension of burning lamps from day to day in the temple in celebration of its deliverance from the abominations of Antiochus. On the other hand it seems more natural to connect the miracle of the closing words of chapter nine with the discourse of chapter eight respecting light. Without determining, therefore, the question of historical connection, we shall be guided by the spiritual significance of the two chapters and treat them as one discourse.

The lesson in the ninth chapter seems the true sequel and close to the previous address. It leads us up to the very highest aspect of light as bringing, not only external illumination, but what is more important, the power to receive it and the internal vision which brings sight as well as light. What is the use of a thousand suns, or a million lamps, to a poor blind beggar? Therefore this is the true climax of His previous teaching.

The Lord heals this poor blind man somewhere near the temple gates. He then makes him an object lesson of deeper spiritual teaching, adding as He performs the miracle, "Neither hath this man sinned, nor his parents: but that the works of God should be made manifest in him. I must work the works of Him that sent Me, while it is day: the night cometh, when no man can work. As long as I am in the world, I am the light of the world" (9:3-5).

The subject of this miracle received something better than even his sight, for we find him springing into the freedom and boldness of a very beautiful faith, standing up in manly vindication of Christ before all the scorn and sarcasm of the Jewish rulers and suffering even excommunication at last rather than compromise his testimony. Jesus comes to him in the hour of his expulsion and reveals Himself in His higher character as the Son of God. The true heart that has followed the light that was previously given still follows Him and comes into all the blessedness of the life of faith.

Jesus closes the chapter with a solemn reference to the readiness of the blind man to receive the light. In contrast with the willful self-conceit and blindness of the Pharisees, but who claimed that they had the light remained in darkness, this simple-hearted beggar, by taking the place of blindness and helplessness, had entered into all the fullness of the light of God.

The first condition, therefore, of spiritual vision is to see our blindness and the insufficiency of natural light and wisdom to bring us into the knowledge of God. This is the deeper teaching of the apostles. This was the lesson which Jewish pride and Jewish wisdom constantly stumbled at in later years and which is hiding from modern culture the truth as it is in Jesus.

"The natural man receiveth not the things of the Spirit of God . . . neither can he know them, because they are spiritually discerned" (1 Corinthians 2:14). A brilliant intellect is as helpless to know Jesus and the gospel without the special illumination of the Holy Ghost as the musical faculty is helpless to study mathematics, or the mathematical faculty unable to write the Iliad of Homer or the Odes of Horace. We must have the mind of Christ even to understand the thoughts and words which Christ has spoken.

# CHAPTER 12

# CHRIST'S DISCOURSES IN THE GOSPEL OF JOHN PART 4

T HIS discourse was delivered at Jerusalem during the Feast of Dedication.

## 7. THE DOOR AND THE SHEPHERD (CHAPTER 10).

As we have already noticed, there is some uncertainty about the twenty-second verse as to whether it looks backward or forward to the discourse which precedes, or that which follows or includes both. For our present purpose, however, as both sections of the discourse refer to the one theme, thus making it ethically but one address, we shall treat it as one discourse.

There is an evident allusion implied in the figure to the conduct of the Jewish rulers and their blindness, selfishness, harshness and cruelty as false guardians of the flock of God which had been entrusted to their keeping, more especially to their harsh treatment of the blind man whom they had just expelled from the synagogue for being true to his conscience and the Saviour. They had proved themselves to be false shepherds, and in contrast with them the Lord now assumes the beautiful title and character which the Old Testament types and prophecies had made so familiar in connection with the hope of the Messiah. He contrasts the Good Shepherd with the selfish hirelings and the thieves and robbers who had usurped the place of shepherds in the flock of God and who so shamefully abused their trust and imposed upon the helpless flock.

There are three divisions in the discourse around which the various thoughts may be clustered: the door (10:7), the shepherd (10:2), the sheep (10:14-15).

Let us keep clearly before our minds the two distinct figures running through this discourse and then all the symbolism will become plain. These are the fold and the flock.

With reference to the fold, Christ is the Door; with reference to the flock, He is the Shepherd. There is a mis-translation in the sixteenth verse of our revised version which tends to confuse the figure and also mislead in the deeper spiritual teaching. The true meaning is, "Other sheep I have which are not of this fold. Them also must I bring, and there shall be," not one fold, but "one flock." There may be many folds, that is, many branches of the visible church among agencies for the nurture of Christians, but there is only one flock.

a. The Door (10:7).

This figure had been used in the symbolism of the tabernacle to denote the curtains by which the priests had access to the Holy Place, which was a type of our fellowship with the Lord and our place of spiritual privilege and blessing. The simple and fundamental idea is that Christ is the only way of access, both into the church and the kingdom. The Church is not the door of Christ, but Christ is the door of the Church and also of salvation in its every stage and its full and final consummation.

He is the door of pardon, of holiness, of access and communion with God; of prayer, of power, of service and of heaven. He is an open door for all who will enter in, and yet He is a closed door, shutting His people in so that they shall never perish, nor shall any pluck them out of His hand. And He is a personal door; not our states or acts, not any ceremony, form or external condition, but union with Himself admits us to all the privileges and immunities of the flock. The one condition of salvation is union with Jesus Christ.

This is the simplicity and glory of Christianity. It has but one door, and the test of all false teachers and false ways is simply this, that they climb up some other way. The touchstone of Christianity is the name of Jesus and its glory His person and His cross.

b. The Shepherd (10:2).

This figure had been invested with peculiar beauty and sacredness in the psalms of David and the prophetic visions of Ezekiel, and possessed a certain divine character which no mere human teacher would ever have dared to assume. Christ's application to Himself of the figure is a virtual claim of divinity. Twice already among His parables had He used this beautiful symbol of His own seeking love. He now applies it, not so much to the seeking of the lost, as to the care and nurture of the flock.

Five things are attributed to the Good Shepherd:

(1) He loves and suffers for His flock. The Good Shepherd giveth His life for His flock. The hireling makes no sacrifice, but seeks only his own interest and safety. The Good Shepherd suffers and even sacrifices His life for His own (10:11, 15, 17).

> The good shepherd giveth his life for the sheep. But he that is an hireling, and not the shepherd, whose own the sheep are not, seeth the wolf coming, and leaveth the sheep, and fleeth: and the wolf catcheth them, and scattereth the sheep. The hireling fleeth, because he is an hireling, and careth not for the sheep. (10:11-13)

> I lay down my life for the sheep. . . . No man taketh it from me, but I lay it down of myself. I have power to lay it down, and I have power to take it again. (10:15, 18).

Thus did He anticipate and prepare His disciples for His approaching death; and thus, voluntarily, did He look forward to it Himself, as a willing sacrifice of love.

(2) He knows His flock personally and calls them by name (10:2-14).

"He calleth his own sheep by name" (10:3). "I am the good shepherd, and know my sheep, and am known of mine" (10:14).

The Oriental shepherd is personally acquainted with each member of his flock. How beautifully Nathan describes this intimacy in 2 Samuel 12:3.

> The poor man had nothing save one little ewe lamb which he had brought up and nourished. It grew up together with him and with his children. It did eat of his own meat,

and drank of his own cup, and lay in his bosom and was unto him as a daughter.

Thus Jesus owns His sheep; for each of us He has a personal love and a personal voice, and, as the mother gives her whole heart to each of her children, although she may have many, so He loves us individually and perfectly. Thus, to His weeping disciple in the garden did He come on the resurrection morning, calling her by her own name. Thus did He adapt himself to the different temperaments of Martha and Mary, and thus each of us has learned to know Him. The voice is different from the written word; He speaks to us all in the latter, but to each of us He has besides a living voice which we may know and follow. It is the revealing of His person and love to the heart.

(3) He leads His flock.

He calleth his own sheep by name, and leadeth them out. And when he putteth forth his own sheep, he goeth before them, and the sheep follow him: for they know his voice. And a stranger will they not follow, but will flee from him: for they know not the voice of strangers. (10:3-5)

He does not merely lead them by His command, but He precedes them in person. There is not a step of the difficult pathway which they must go but He has already gone before them all the way. There is not a hard place still where He pushes them out in advance but they may always hear His voice in front saying, "Arise, let us go hence." The personal companionship of Christ, and His direct and conscious guidance in every step of our pathway, is the most certain and delightful fact of Christian experience.

(4) He feeds them, supplying all their needs and leading them into the fullness of His grace (10:9-10).

By me if any man enter in, he shall be saved, and shall go in and out, and find pasture. . . . I am come that they might have life, and that they might have it more abundantly. (10:9-10)

"He maketh me to lie down in green pastures: He leadeth me by the waters of rest" (Psalm 23:2, author's paraphrase). His word and its precious promises, His Holy Spirit, His tender consolation, His public ordinances and all their blessed fellowship, instruction and inspiration; these are the pastures of His love and bounty, in which we find not only life, but the life more abundantly.

(5) He keeps them, guards them, defends them and will never let them fall from His hands or be lost from His flock (John 10:28-29).

> I give unto them eternal life; and they shall never perish, neither shall any man pluck them out of my hand. My Father, which gave them me, is greater than all; and no man is able to pluck them out of my Father's hand (10:28-29).

Locked in the double clasp of the Father and of the Son, the trusting soul is safe forever if it only heeds this simple condition, "My sheep hear my voice . . . and they follow me" (10:27). There is a cast-iron way of stating the doctrine of the saint's security which would seem to sanction rash and unholy confidence. God's Word is never spoken in a one-sided manner so as to encourage confidence in any course of disobedience and sin; but for those who have fled for refuge to the hope set before us and are humbly abiding in Him, there is indeed strong consolation and a hope which is an anchor of the soul, both sure and steadfast, and which entereth into that within the veil.

  c. The flock.

  (1) They hear His voice (10:3-27).

The sheep hear His voice. "My sheep hear my voice" (10:27). "Ye believe not, because ye are not of my sheep, as I said unto you" (10:26). This is the mark of true sheep, they hearken to the shepherd's voice and are willing to be led and taught. This hearkening spirit, both through the Old Testament and the New, is the very secret of the Lord and the mark of His spiritual followers.

  (2) They follow the Shepherd (10:4-5, 27).

The sheep follow Him for they know His voice. "My sheep hear my voice . . . and they follow me" (10:27). This expression includes the whole life of humble and holy obedience to the commandments and leadings of the Lord. It implies His personal presence and leadership. We do not have to walk alone, but He goes before. It makes the way easy to have only to follow. This was the first word to the disciples in the first chapter of John, and this was the last word to Peter in the twenty-first, "Follow thou me."

(3) They know Him (10:4, 14-15).

The sheep follow Him for they know His voice, and a stranger will they not follow, for they know not the voice of strangers. "I . . . know my sheep, and am known of mine. As the Father knoweth me, even so know I the Father" (10:14-15); that is, we know the Shepherd as He knows the Father. Our personal intimacy with Jesus is the same as His with His Father in heaven.

The translation of the fifteenth verse obscures this thought a little. It ought to read, "I am known of Mine as the Father knoweth Me and as I know the Father." These thoughts lead us into depths and heights which as yet His disciples could not understand. We do not wonder therefore to read in the sixth verse, "This parable spake Jesus unto them: but they understood not what things they were which he spake unto them."

But the time came when the same apostle John could use that word know with even a deeper fullness than this chapter anywhere expresses, and say of the flock: "Ye have known him that is from the beginning. . . . Ye have an unction from the Holy One, and ye know all things" (1 John 2:14, 20). "We know that we are of the truth, and shall assure our hearts before him" (3:19). "We know that he abideth in us, by the Spirit which he hath given us" (3:24). "We have known and believed the love that God hath to us" (4:16). "We know that we have passed from death unto life" (3:14). "We know that we have the petitions that we desired of Him" (5:15). "We know that we are of God, and the whole world lieth in wickedness. And we know that the Son of God is come, and hath given us an understanding, that we may know him that is true, and we are in him that is true, even in his Son Jesus Christ. This is the true God and eternal life" (5:19-20).

This discourse has reference not only to the individual believer, but also to the entire flock, and contains a beautiful reference to the time when its scattered fragments shall be all united, Jew and Gentile, out of every nation, and class and age of time. "And there shall be one fold, and one shepherd" (John 10:16).

"For the Lamb which is in the midst of the throne shall feed them, and shall lead them unto living fountains of waters: and God shall wipe away all tears from their eyes" (Revelation 7:17).

This beautiful discourse, instead of touching the hearts of His enemies, only stung them to fiercer exasperations. It was followed by a malignant attack upon Him and an attempt to stone Him in the temple. He escaped through the same supernatural power by which He had already evaded their fury more than once and departed from Jerusalem to Perea for the last stage of His Jewish ministry.

## 8. THE GLORY OF THE CROSS (John 12:20-36).

The occasion of this discourse was the arrival of certain Greeks who had come to attend the Feast of the Passover to ask for an introduction to Jesus through Philip. They may have had some slight acquaintance with him, or he may have had, perhaps, some Gentile blood in him. Philip consults with Andrew, and then together they go to the Master and tell Him of the request.

It seems to make a profound impression upon His heart, and doubtless He sees in it the type and beginning of the conversion of the Gentiles, through the gospel, which the Christian age is soon to usher in. The innumerable multitudes who are to follow in their train passed before Him in vision. Perhaps the prospect of these ransomed millions, saved through His suffering and death, lifts His spirit into exulting joy even under the immediate shadow of the cross itself. He exclaims, "The hour is come, that the Son of man should be glorified" (12:23). He then proceeds, in profound and beautiful language, to unfold the great principle of death and resurrection, of which His life was to be the greatest expression. First, He traces it even in the laws of nature. Then He applies it both to His disciples and to Himself.

a. The principle of death and resurrection in the natural world.

"Except a corn of wheat fall into the ground and die, it abideth alone: but if it die, it bringeth forth much fruit"(12:24). This is the law of natural life. We see it in the decay of winter and revival of spring; we see it in the chrysalis and in the butterfly; we see it in the bulb of autumn and the lily of spring; we see it in the buried seed and the harvest resurrection.

> Life, evermore, is fed by death,
>> And joy, by agony,
> And that a rose may breathe its breath
>> Something must die.

b. The application of this principle to all discipleship.

"He that loveth his life shall lose it; and he that hateth his life in this world shall keep it unto life eternal" (12:25).

Every follower of the Master must be willing to rise to life and kingliness by way of the cross, by the death of self and by the portals of suffering. The word *life* here is expressed by two Greek terms having quite a different sense. The first means our lower life; the second, our higher and divine life. He that loveth the former shall lose the latter, but he that yields it for the higher shall gain the life eternal. The first might be translated "soul"; it is the Greek *psyche*. He that loveth his own soul shall lose it; he that hateth it shall keep it unto life eternal.

Not only must Christian life be animated by the spirit of self-sacrifice, it must really begin in the renunciation and death of self in its very germ, in the surrender of our natural self to Jesus and in the reception of the new resurrection life in fellowship with Him. We can then say, "I am crucified with Christ: nevertheless I live, yet not I, but Christ liveth in me" (Galatians 2:20). Not only must it have its source in this great principle, but it must, all the way, enter into fellowship with Christ's sufferings. "If any man serve me, let him follow me; and where I am, there shall also my servant be" (John 12:26).

But the cross is not forever; there is a glorious and everlasting reversion. "If any man serve me . . . him will my Father honour" (12:26). "If we be dead with him, we shall also live with him: If we suffer, we shall also reign with him" (2 Timothy 2:11-12). "The sufferings of this present time are not worthy to be compared with the glory which shall be revealed in us" (Romans 8:18).

c. The application of this principle to Himself.

He, too, must bear the cross in all its terrible reality; and for a moment, as the realization of it touches His sensitive spirit, He shrinks from the awful vision and cries, "Now is my soul troubled; and what shall I say? Father, save me from this hour" (John 12:27).

It was the instinctive recoil of His humanity from the cup of trembling; it was the foretaste of Gethsemane, as that was the foretaste of Calvary. But it was only a moment's recoil, nor was it really accepted by His consecrated will. Instantly He answers His own cry, "But for this cause came I unto this hour. Father, glorify thy name" (12:27-28). And His holy will is still immaculately held on the altar of sacrifice in a very real sense. It is with Him the hour of sacrifice and death.

There are moments when we live over in the soul all the history of coming hours of anguish, and this was such a moment. But immediately the shadow is illumined by the glory beyond.

(1) First, we have the Father's witness to His sacrifice by an audible voice from heaven in response to His prayer, proclaiming, "I have both glorified it, and will glorify it again" (12:28). This is the highest glory of the cross, that it honors the Father and glorifies His name. It is the sublimest exhibition of His justice, holiness, wisdom and love. It is the one offering which satisfies His heart with the perfect obedience of His beloved Son and the all-sufficient ransom for a lost and guilty world.

In these Greeks He saw the prototypes of the world's coming myriads, as they have been coming, and shall still come to Him for salvation; until, at length, an innumerable company that no man can number, out of all nations, and kindreds, and people and tongues shall gather around the throne, and before the Lamb. Clothed with white robes and palms in their hands, they will shout, "Salvation to Him that sitteth upon the throne, and unto the Lamb" (Revelations 7:10, author's paraphrase).

(2) The cross is also the judgment of this world (John 12:31).

"Now," He cries, "is the judgment of this world" (12:31). Not only was it the hour when the world was revealed in the deepest and darkest element of its wickedness and hatred toward God, but it was literally the hour when, in the person of the Substitute, the judgment of heaven was really passed upon sinful men. And for all who accept the atonement of Jesus the day of judgment is really passed so far as their former sins are concerned. The Lord Jesus Himself declares of them that they "shall not come into condemnation; but [have] passed from death unto life" (5:24).

(3) It is also the way of assured victory over Satan.

This is another of the glories of the cross, that through death it has destroyed him that had the power of death, that is the devil (Hebrews 2:16). The very act by which he sought to destroy the Redeemer and the hopes of men has ruined the foundations of his kingdom and sealed his everlasting fate. Never did Satan do a rasher deed than when he incited Judas and Pilate to crucify the Son of God. By His death Jesus has spoiled principalities and powers and made a show of them openly, triumphing over them in His cross (Colossians 2:15). The strong figure of the apostle implies that Satan has been hung up as a scarecrow on the cross of Calvary, with his head pierced with the nails of crucifixion. We all may know henceforth that he is a slain and conquered foe.

d. The crowning glory of the cross is its attractive power to draw all men unto Jesus for salvation.

This was the meaning of His joyful cry, "If I be lifted up from the earth, will draw all men unto me" (12:32). The lifting up referred, primarily, to His crucifixion but also might include His resurrection and His exhibition in the preaching of the gospel, for it is only as we lift up a crucified and risen Saviour that we shall ever be honored to draw men unto Him.

Soon after this beautiful discourse Jesus withdrew Himself from the people, hiding Himself, as it is expressed, from them, and adding the solemnly tender warning, "Yet a little while is the light is with you. Walk while ye have the light, lest darkness come upon you:, for he that walketh in darkness knoweth not whither he goeth. While ye have light, believe in the light, that ye may be the children of light" (12:35-36). And to those who believed on Him in secret and were afraid to confess because of others, He gave this parting admonition:

> He that believeth on me, believeth not on me, but on him that sent me. . . He that rejecteth me, and receiveth not my words, hath one that judgeth him: the word that I have spoken, the same shall judge him in the last day. For I have not spoken of myself; but the Father which sent me, he gave me a commandment, what I should say, and what I should speak. And I know that his commandment

is life everlasting: whatsoever I speak therefore, even as the Father said unto me, so I speak. (12:44, 48-50)

This solemn thought was enough to lift them above all the thought and fears of men. They were dealing with the Son of God, with the word of God, with the issues of judgment; they were receiving not only the wisdom of a man and the kind and Christian words of a divine messenger, but the commandment of the Father and a decisive message on the acceptance of which their eternal destiny should be settled before the throne.

The offer of salvation comes to us not merely as a well-meaning opportunity, but as an authoritative command. God commands us to receive life everlasting. The law of faith is the test now of judgment and destiny, and in the day of His coming there shall be two classes, described in the earlier verses of this Gospel by the solemn words, "He that believeth on him is not condemned: but he that believeth not is condemned already. . . . [and] shall not see life; but the wrath of God abideth on him: (3:18,36).

# CHAPTER 13

# CHRIST'S DISCOURSES
# IN THE GOSPEL OF JOHN
# PART 5

This entire discourse was given while they sat at the table in the Upper Room. It is naturally divided into six sections by the six questions to Him; each contains His answer.

*9. PARTING WORDS OF JESUS AT THE TABLE (13:12–16:31).*

a. His own question to the disciples, "Know ye what I have done to you?" (13:12).

The answer to this contains His beautiful teachings concerning humility and brotherly love, as expressed in the example He had just set them by washing their feet.

> If I then, your Lord and Master, have washed your feet; ye also ought to wash one another's feet. For I have given you an example, that ye should do as I have done to you. Verily, verily . . . the servant is not greater than his lord; neither He that is sent greater than he that sent him. If ye know these things, happy are ye if ye do them. (13:14-17)

b. The question of John, "Lord, who is it?" (13:25).

This question refers to the betrayer. Jesus answers it by giving the sign to Judas and so addressing him that the betrayer is forced to withdraw from the presence of the Master and the disciples. This is what Jesus desired before speaking His words of tender and confidential farewell. He could not bear the pressure of this hideous consciousness of treachery and evil, and yet He did it so tenderly that the act was Judas' own.

His departure is followed by a solemn and emphatic declaration, suggested by what He knows of the dark purpose of the traitor: "Now is the Son of man glorified, and God is glorified in him" (13:31). He does not say now is the Son of Man *crucified;* but above all the shame and anguish of the cross He sees the spanning rainbow of the glory it will bring to His Father and the subsequent recompense which it is also to bring to Him, for He adds, "If God be glorified in him, God shall also glorify him" (13:32).

Then there falls upon His loving heart the shadow of the separation which it is to involve for His beloved disciples, "Yet a little while I am with you. . . . Whither I go, ye cannot come" (13:33). But this separation is to bind them closer to each other and bring them that blessing which will be next to His own presence and love: the bond of brotherly love. And so, in this way, the new commandment of Christianity is instituted and promulgated. "A new commandment I give unto you, That ye love one another"; not, as the old law expressed, as you love yourselves, but "as I have loved you" (13:34).

This is indeed the divine principle of Christianity, and was, by the admission of its enemies, among the divinest causes of its successful progress in the early centuries. It is not a natural affection, based on congenial affinities and qualities, but born of the Holy Spirit, imparted from the heart of Jesus, and measured only by His own measureless love.

c. The question of Peter, "Lord, whither goest thou? . . . Why cannot I follow thee now?" (13:36-37).

The first answer Jesus gave was an assurance to the impulsive disciple that he shall yet follow Him whither He goes. It must have been a comfort in view of all the words and experiences that followed. The next reply is a solemn intimation of his own great sin. It must have fallen like a shock of unutterable and perhaps of long—continued silence on the little group. "Verily, verily, I say unto thee, The cock shall not crow, till thou hast denied me thrice" (13:38).

The effect of these three tremendous announcements, that one should betray Him, another, even His boldest follower, deny Him, and He Himself soon pass out of sight where they cannot even follow Him, we can easily believe was a shock of intense distress and almost complete prostration to the little band of disciples. Dark shadows must have gathered on their faces, and perhaps their eyes were filled with tears of anxious grief.

It was then that the Master spoke again and uttered those sweetest words of consolation perhaps ever expressed by Him, in which He most fully answers Peter's question, "Whither goest thou?"

> Let not your heart be troubled: ye believe in God, believe also in me. In my Father's house are many mansions: if it were not so, I would have told you. I go to prepare a place for you. . . . I will come again, and receive you unto myself; that where I am, there ye may be also. And whither I go ye know, and the way ye know. (14:1-4).

(1) He comforts their hearts by sympathy, with the words, "Let not your hearts be troubled" (14:1). The tone in which they were doubtless uttered was meant to cheer them by the very tenderness of His love and sympathy for them, even before He spake a single word of faith or hope.

Still that loving sympathy is throbbing in His heart toward every one of His troubled children. He would shield us from our heart troubles and pillow our heads upon His gentle bosom. If the heart can but rise above its troubles, they will not overwhelm us, even as the billows of the ocean cannot submerge the struggling ship so long as the hatchways are closed and the water does not enter the hold. Christ, and Christ alone, can keep the heart victorious and still in the wildest conflict.

(2) He comforts them by encouraging their faith, "Believe in God," He says; "believe also in me" (14:1). It is not, ye believe in God, but a command. Over against every difficult place let us write the words, "but God." Let us remember that we have a divine Protector and Shield, but let us also add to the transcendent thought of God this sweet thought of Jesus, "Believe also in Me." Let us clothe His sweetness with the divine omnipotence, and let us color the divine omnipotence with the soft light of His love.

This is the Lamb in the midst of the throne, the gentleness in the midst of the Almightiness. "Believe also in Me."

Faith is the true source of abiding comfort. Sympathy alone is not enough, we must also trust. And the first resting place of our trust is His person. "Believe in God."

Then He adds the following words to lift their faith to the throne where He is about to ascend and the work on which He is immediately to enter in their behalf. "I go to prepare a place for you" (14:2).

Faith not only rests upon the person of Christ, but also loves to dwell upon the place where He has gone, the right hand of God, and the work which He is doing representing us and preparing our future home. And once more He reveals the way by which they are still to have communion with Him even in His absence and in a little while to rise to meet Him. "Whither I go ye know, and the way ye know" (14:4).

It is not enough to know that He is there, and there for us, but we also need to know how we may communicate with Him and ultimately follow Him. This, too, He says, we know. And a little later He tells them it is He Himself. Faith thus rests upon Jesus, the way of access to God, and if we will only thus believe our hearts will never be troubled.

(3) He comforts them not only by faith, but also by hope.

He intimates first that He Himself is coming again for them in a little while. This is the Church's chief hope, oft obscure and even forgotten, but her one supreme consolation—the coming of her Lord. "I will come again, and receive you unto myself" (14:3). This is not death, but the brighter, better hope of His own personal return.

(4) He gives them a glimpse of the glory that awaits them at His coming and speaks of the mansions, the Father's house and the place prepared.

All this is suggested by the figure of the Father's house, the metropolis of this magnificent universe, the mansions with which His infinite power and glory will adorn that celestial city and the preparation which His loving hands are about to give to their future home. We may be assured there will be nothing wanting which thoughtful love could plan, and all this may well suggest a vision of glory and happiness which should dry their tears and fill their hearts with hope and consolation.

There is still another thought suggested by the word "many" which hints at the happy reunion which His coming will bring with the many that are linked with their affections and hopes. It shall not be a solitary grandeur, but a restoration of broken ties and a healing of broken hearts in everlasting love.

And there is a still finer hint in one sentence, which suggests an inexpressible meaning of comfort, "If it were not so, I would have told you" (14:2). But how much this covers: hopes that we scarcely dare to utter but still feel that He has not forgotten, and a whole world of unrevealed and unutterable satisfactions which our bursting hearts cannot regulate.

d. The question of Thomas (14:5-7).

"Lord, we know not whither thou goest; and how can we know the way?" (14:5).

Thomas is a natural doubter, partly because of his ardent love. His heart takes so intense a hold on things that he cannot bear to be deceived. He, therefore, cannot rest in any indefiniteness but must know without doubt or vagueness, not only the certainty of these bright hopes, but the very way by which they are to be fulfilled. This Jesus answers by giving a more emphatic announcement of His own personality, as the one answer both to this and all their questionings. "I am the way," He says, "the truth, and the life" (14:6).

It is not in a physical or material manifestation that you are to be led into these hopes and maintain this communication with Me, but through your spiritual union and fellowship with Me, for I am not only the Way, but I am also the Truth and the Life. And as you know Me and abide in communion with Me, you are also to know the Father and have access to His presence. You are to know of the truth of My teachings and the deepest experiences of spiritual life. For I am also the Life as well as the Truth and the Way.

The first of these beautiful expressions may well describe our justification; the second, our deeper teaching; and the third, our deeper life in Christ. We are saved by simply coming to Him and becoming united to Him.

There is no way but He, and there is no need of any way to Him for He Himself is the way. And so, as regards our higher teaching, it is not truth in the abstract that we need to know, but the truth as it is in Jesus. He is the substance of all the teachings of the Old Testament and the deeper revelations of the New. They all terminate with Him. The object of each is to reveal Him and have us know Him as our personal light and the substance of all knowledge and wisdom. And so of our life, whether it be of soul or body. It is not an impartation from Him, but it is His own very life, shed abroad in us, sustaining us by constant dependence upon Himself, so that, as He says a little later, "Because I live, ye shall live also" (14:19).

e. The question of Philip (14:8-21).

"Lord, show us the Father, and it sufficeth us"

This whole passage is, in some sense, the answer to this question.

(1) He tells them that He is the manifestation of the Father and that all His works on earth have been through the energy of the Father working in Him. He expresses surprise that Philip should not yet have known Him in His divine character and relationship.

(2) He tells them that he is about to go to the Father. He shall still reveal His power and grace, no less than when on earth, but even more mightily through His disciples. Just now as He represents the Father on earth, so they, then, shall represent Him. "And greater works than these shall [ye] do; because I go unto my Father" (14:12).

(3) He tells them that the answers to their prayers are about to be revealed after His ascension. They will be the evidence to them of His union with the Father. "Whatsoever ye shall ask in my name, that will I do, that the Father may be glorified in the Son" (14:13).

(4) The Holy Spirit, who is about to descend upon them, will be another proof of His union with the Father. He will come from the Father at His intercession and will dwell in them, both as the Revealer of the Father and of the Son, and as the Representative of the Godhead henceforth on earth.

(5) The Comforter.

The Holy Ghost shall not be so distinct from Him that He shall be another presence, for He shall be the Spirit which has hitherto dwelt in Christ. He shall come as the Spirit of Christ and thus bring the personal presence of Christ in abiding union and conscious fellowship. He shall reveal to the soul the person of Jesus and His relation to the Father with glorious vividness and blessedness. He says, "I will not leave you comfortless: I will come to you" (14:18). That is, through the coming of the Comforter. And then He adds,

> At that day ye shall know that I am in my Father, and ye in me, and I in you. He that hath my commandments, and keepeth them, he it is that loveth me: and he that loveth me shall be loved of my Father, and I will love him, and will manifest myself unto him. (14:20-21)

Thus the question of Philip is fully answered. Not only does Jesus say that the Father is in His own incarnate person, but, after His ascension, He is to send the Holy Spirit to reveal Himself to them in closer intimacy and to bring the presence of the Father Himself into their hearts so that they shall know that He is in the Father and they in Him and He in them. Thus the whole mystery of the Trinity will be revealed in the living experience of the consecrated heart. This, indeed, is the only way in which any soul can ever fully grasp and find comfort and support in the doctrine of the Trinity.

As a speculation, it is as cold as it is lofty; but as an experience, brought to the heart by the Holy Spirit through the indwelling presence of Jesus, it is a three-fold cord of infinite joy and everlasting love.

f. The question of Jude's (14: 22-24).

"Lord, how is it that thou wilt manifest thyself unto us, and not unto the world?" (14:22).

First, He tells them the very secret of this manifestation is obedience and love. The world cannot, therefore, know Him, because it neither loves nor obeys Him. But he that will obey Him shall know this, not as an occasional flash of light and glory, but as an abiding joy, making the heart a literal heaven where the Father, Son and Holy Ghost erect their throne and make their continual abode. "If a man love me, he will keep my words: and my Father will love him, and we will come unto him, and make our abode with him" (14:23).

g. Summing up of all these teachings and closing benediction as He rises from the table (14:25-31).

First, He tells them that these parting words have been spoken to them in view of His separation from them; but that these and all other things which they shall need to know, and many of which they may indeed forget, will be brought to their remembrance and more fully revealed by the manifestation of the Holy Ghost. He is about to come in His very name, as His Substitute and Successor, to represent Him and to finish His work. "He shall teach you all things, and bring all things to your remembrance, whatsoever I have said unto you" (14:26). Therefore, although there may be much at present that they cannot fully comprehend, and much they may fear they shall forget, yet He shall be their faithful and patient Teacher, and all that now seems strange shall be made perfectly plain.

Next, He gives them His parting benediction and bequest, His own divine peace. "Peace I leave with you, my peace I give unto you: not as the world giveth, give I unto you. Let not your heart be troubled, neither let it be afraid" (14:27). They had seen this wonderful peace in Him and felt its majestic power, now He breathes it into their very hearts and leaves it to all of His disciples as His Last Will and Testament—the "peace of God which passeth all understanding . . . to keep [their] hearts and minds through Christ Jesus" (Philippians 4:7).

Then He tries to rouse them to the still higher thought of love to Him and awaken in their breasts the unselfish consideration of His needs and feelings in this trying hour. "If ye loved me," He says, "ye would rejoice, because I said, I go unto the Father" (John 14:28).

There is no higher consolation to the troubled heart than to be lifted out of itself and think of the greater sufferings of others. If they had only realized their Master's condition and immediate prospects, their own troubles would have seemed like a dream. They would have thrown their arms about Him and cried, "Master, let us comfort thee, let not thy heart be troubled."

Then, with a brief reference to the conflict which is just coming, the victory which He is already sharing, and the solemn consideration of His Father's will and glory (which is His chief support), He slowly rises from the table and summons them to follow with the words which might well look forward to every future place of difficulty and duty. "Arise, let us go hence" (14:31).

The whole of this beautiful chapter might be summed up under two divisions: First, His going, and second, His coming again. His going is to prepare a place for them, to open a way for them, to intercede for them with the Father, to work through them from the throne His greater works and to send to them the Comforter to represent Him and continue His work. His coming again looks forward ultimately to His glorious second advent (14:3), but also includes His personal indwelling in their hearts (14:18, 20-21, 23) and His giving to them as His ever-present legacy of blessing His own perfect peace (14:27).

# CHAPTER 14

# *CHRIST'S DISCOURSES IN THE GOSPEL OF JOHN PART 6*

THIS long discourse consists of three parts: The parable of the vine and the branches and its applications (15:1-25).

Fuller promise of the coming of the Comforter (15:26—16:15).

Concluding conversation between the disciples and the Lord about various questions.

*10. PARTING WORDS ON THE WAY FROM THE TABLE TO THE GARDEN (John 15—16).*

a. The Vine and the Branches.

The occasion of this discourse may have been their passing through the court of the temple and observing the magnificent carving of the vine in stone which was one of the most remarkable decorations of the building. Or it may have been suggested by the overhanging vines by the roadside as they passed down to the valley of the Kedron, or the burning of the withered branches and pruning of the vineyards in the open places as they went out of the city. It was not a new figure, but drawn by Him from the beautiful imagery of the psalms and the prophets (Psalm 80:8; Isaiah 5:1; Jeremiah 2:21; Ezekiel 15:2).

The most valuable, perhaps, of the products of the vegetable creation, God has chosen it as the most significant figure of Christ and His relation to His people. The devil has tried to prostitute it, perhaps for this very reason, to the most unholy and wicked purposes.

(1) Union with Christ as represented by this figure.

(a)Let us observe that the vine consists not only of the stem, but of the branches; so Christ identifies Himself with all His members and counts them part of Himself. We are of the very same substance as our living Head, and partake of His own personal life.

(b) The fruit is borne not by the stem, but by the branches, and, especially, by the little branches. So the Lord Jesus did not, in His own personal ministry, bring many souls to God, but left the most glorious fruit of the gospel to be gathered by His disciples. He still honors His feeblest members by permitting us to bring forth much fruit.

(c) The great essential of Christian life is to be united to Jesus. "Without me ye can do nothing" (John 15:5).

Two things constitute this union. The first is expressed by the words, "in me" (15:4). This denotes our faith in Christ for salvation and our union with Him in justification. The second, "I in you" (15:4) expresses a closer union, even His personal coming into the heart in the hour of our full surrender to abide in us by the Holy Spirit, as our Lord and life.

This is the secret of sanctification, communion, power and fruitfulness.

(d) We must abide in this union and communion. It is not enough that it be formed, it must be maintained, moment by moment, in watchful, obedient dependence and fellowship.

(e) In connection with our abiding in Christ, it is necessary that there should be much faithful divine discipline. Therefore we read of the pruning of the vine and the Father's thoughtful, patient care as the heavenly Husbandman.

(f) On our part there must be obedience if we would abide in Christ. "If ye keep my commandments, ye shall abide in my love" (15:10). And again, "Ye are my friends, if ye do whatsoever I command you" (15:14). And again, "This is my commandment, That ye love one another, as I have loved you" (15:12).

(2) The fruits of union with Christ.

(a) They are fruits, not works of the flesh and the will. They spring spontaneously and delightfully from the life within, just as the vine bears fruit without effort and the fruit seems to grow for very gladness.

(b) The first of these fruits is holiness. "Now ye are clean through the word which I have spoken unto you" (15:3). All true holiness must spring from the indwelling life of Christ.

(c) The next fruit is holy usefulness. This is expressed by the figure of much fruit, for fruit is reproduction—some thirty, some sixty and some an hundredfold. "Herein is my Father glorified, that ye bear much fruit" (15:8).

(d) The next fruit is answered prayer. "If ye abide in Me, and My words abide in you, ye shall ask what ye will, and it shall be done unto you" (15:7).

(e) Fullness of joy. "These things have I spoken unto you, that my joy might remain in you, and that your joy might be full" (15:11). If His life is in us, His joy will fill us. And His joy is fullness of joy.

(f) The fellowship of His sufferings. If we are one with Him, the world will hate us, as it hated Him (15:18-21); but we will not shrink from His cross or seek to be greater than our Lord, or more exempt from persecution and suffering, for trial will be sweet as it comes with the recollection that we are suffering with Jesus. We shall be also glorified together.

b. The Comforter (15:26—16:15).

In the previous discourse, He had referred to the coming of the Holy Spirit as their teacher and guide, but here He unfolds His special ministry with more explicitness.

(1) The necessity and importance of His coming.

His presence is so essential to the next stage of their experience and work that it is even expedient that their beloved Master go away in order that He may come. Anything that could require the withdrawal of such a friend must be valuable indeed. And yet, the Holy Spirit's presence with the Church is better than the continued physical presence of the Lord Jesus would have been. For, in the first place, it is an internal and not an external presence. Further, He is omnipresent, not limited, as the visible person of Christ, to one place, but equally accessible to all God's people wherever they may be and at all times. Moreover, the mission of the Spirit is to act as the Executive of the divine plan of redemption. The time was now come when this stage of the work must follow the personal ministry and accomplished sacrifice of Jesus Himself.

(2) The mission of the Comforter with respect to the Father.

He was to proceed from the Father in response to the prayer of Jesus. "I will pray the Father, and he shall give you another Comforter" (14:16). "When the Comforter is come, whom I will send unto you from the Father, even the spirit of truth, which proceedeth from the Father, he shall testify of me" (15:26).

(3) The mission of the Comforter with respect to the Son.

He was to come in the name of Christ (14:26).

He was to be the very Spirit that had dwelt in Christ. As has been beautifully expressed, He comes to us not in His essential deity but colored by the humanity of Jesus in whom He has resided. And He comes to unite us with the person of Jesus. "At that day ye shall know that I am in my Father, and ye in me, and I in you" (14:20).

He comes to testify of Jesus, to make His presence real and vivid to our consciousness and to illuminate our spirit with the revelation of Jesus Christ in all His fullness. "He shall testify of me. . . . He shall glorify me; for he shall receive of mine, and shall shew it unto you" (15:26; 16:14).

The Holy Spirit is to Christ what the atmosphere of our globe is to the sun. We do not see the atmosphere, but the light of the sun, yet that light would be invisible but for the atmospheric medium through which it is diffused. The viewless air brings to us the vision of the sun, and so the Holy Ghost, hiding His own personality behind the person of Jesus, brings Him into our consciousness and life to glorify Him.

The telescope may be beautiful and costly in its construction, but it would be a mistake for a visitor to the great Observatory of yonder Sierra Nevada mountains to concentrate his whole attention on the superb telescope which the munificence of a wealthy patron of science has erected. Much wiser and grander would it be to use the telescope to gaze upon yonder celestial spheres, and see, not the medium of vision, but the heavenly worlds themselves.

Let us honor the Holy Spirit just because He does not seek to honor Himself; but we shall ever please Him best, and have His most gracious approbation, when we unite our gaze with Him upon the face of Jesus.

(4) The mission of the Comforter with respect to the disciples.

Already, in the preceding discourse, has He been revealed as their indwelling Teacher and Monitor. Here He is represented still more fully in this respect as the patient and gentle Guide. He will supplement the present instructions of the Master by such fuller unfoldings of the truth as they may be able to bear from time to time, especially the truths respecting the future and the second coming of the Lord—the whole prophetic horizon which was to be opened to their view a little later. "He will guide you into all truth . . . and he will show you things to come" (16:13). He was also to be to them the spirit of testimony. "He shall testify of me: And ye also shall bear witness, because ye have been with me from the beginning" (15:26-27).

(5) The mission of the Comforter with respect to the world.

> And when he is come, he will reprove the world of sin, and of righteousness, and of judgment: Of sin, because they believe not on me; Of righteousness, because I go to my Father, and ye see me no more; Of judgment, because the prince of this world is judged. (16:8-11)

His first work upon the hearts of sinners is to convict them of sin, the deepest need of the unconverted heart; and the special sin, for which He arraigns the human conscience, is that which is to be the ground of final condemnation, the rejection of Jesus Christ.

Next, His work is to reveal to the soul the righteousness of Christ as the ground of its justification and the source of its sanctification, and enable it to accept the righteousness of God as witnessed by the resurrection of Jesus Christ in both these aspects.

The exact meaning of the third specification of His work has been variously interpreted. Some apply it symbolically and literally to the future judgment. It seems a little difficult, however, to connect, intelligibly, with this, the next sentence, with regard to the prince of this world being judged. It would seem relevant and clear to apply this to the revelation of Christ's second coming; the next great theme of the Gospel and its glorious result in the judging and casting out of Satan and the power of his kingdom.

It would seem to unfold, also, the idea of the world and the devil as now already judged by the Lord, and, therefore, to be treated by the disciple of Christ as a conquered foe. This is the closing echo of this very discourse: "Be of good cheer, I have overcome the world" (16:33). The world and the devil, its master, are already judged, and the judgment will be made manifest in all its fullness at His second coming. We are, therefore, to be separated from it as a forbidden world of evil, and to testify against it. We are not to fear it in its opposition and persecution, or its malignant and mighty prince, the devil, but to treat him as a conquered foe.

All this the Spirit reveals to the soul, after convicting it of sin and righteousness; leading it out of the world, giving it victory over temptation and inspiring the blessed hope of Christ's second coming and the new world of righteousness and glory.

c. Closing conversation between Christ and His disciples (16:16-33).

The remaining utterances of this discourse are somewhat broken by the questionings of His disciples. The first subject referred to is His expected separation from them and His speedy reappearance to them. His own remark, "A little while, and ye shall not see me: and again, a little while, and ye shall see me" (16:16), had perplexed them. He tenderly anticipates their question and more fully explains His meaning in verses 20-22.

He plainly intimates in these words His approaching death and the sorrow it will bring them, as well as the malignant triumph of the hostile world. But it will be followed immediately by His reappearance to them; a joy, which, thenceforth, shall never pass away.

This dark hour, that is approaching like the anguish of a travailing woman, is but the birth throe of a new creation which is about to come—even the birth of the Church of Christ which is to emerge from the cross and the resurrection and go forth into a cloudless and everlasting day.

The reference is, undoubtedly, to His appearance to them after His resurrection and to the exalted fellowship and privileges into which they are then to be raised. He proceeds next to unfold these privileges:

> In that day ye shall ask me nothing. Verily, verily, I say unto you, Whatsoever ye shall ask the Father in my name, he will give it you. Hitherto, have ye asked nothing in my name: ask, and ye shall receive, that your joy may be full. . . At that day ye shall ask in my name: and I say not unto you, that I will pray the Father for you: For the Father Himself loveth you, because ye have loved me, and have believed that I came out from God. (16:23-24, 26-27)

The first word translated *ask* in verse 23 does not mean to pray, but to inquire about matters with respect to which they are in perplexity. He means that in the coming day, the light will be so plain and clear, that they will not need to inquire as they do now. "What is this that He saith? We cannot tell what He saith." They shall plainly understand His will and teachings and His Father's love.

And, as to prayer, they shall have a higher place of access and confidence for they shall ask in His name, even as He asks, which they have not yet been able to do because His redemption work was not complete and His heavenly priesthood, in their behalf, had not begun. But henceforth He shall be at the Father's side in their interests. Their petitions shall be received at the heavenly throne even as His own. Nor will He need to plead for them as for strangers, or aliens, for the Father Himself loves them, even as He loves His Son.

His intercession is not so much to propitiate an angry Father and constrain from His reluctant hands the answer to His people's prayers, as that He is to be the channel through whom the answer will come. He will be the Mediator who receives our petitions as they ascend to heaven, in their imperfection and ignorance, purifying them with His holy intercession and then presenting them with the added incense of His own merits as His own very prayers.

There is one more word, and then this tender discourse closes. There is a touch of deep sorrow in its tone, but it soon rises to the notes of triumph. "Do ye now believe?" (16:31). He answers their honest but superficial confession. "Behold, the hour cometh . . . that ye shall be scattered, every man to his own, and shall leave me alone" (16:32). Thus was the dark shadow of Gethsemane anticipated; but He quickly rises and adds, "Yet I am not alone, because the Father is with me" (16:32).

And then, looking forward to their Gethsemane, too, He tenderly says, "In the world ye shall have tribulation" (16:33). They, too, shall have their crosses and their conflicts, but their one source of rest and victory is Himself and His triumph for them. "These things I have spoken unto you, that in me ye might have peace. In the world ye shall have tribulation: but be of good cheer; I have overcome the world" (16:33). That victory is the pledge of ours; as we cry out for strength, His answer ever is, "I have overcome for you." And so,

> As surely as He overcame,
>    And triumphed once for you,
> So, surely, ye that trust His name,
>    Shall triumph in Him, too.

## CHAPTER 15

# *CHRIST'S DISCOURSES.*
# *IN THE GOSPEL OF JOHN*
# *PART 7*

**P**ERHAPS on the brink of the Kedron, or possibly even within the temple courts before they finally withdrew, these last words of love were spoken. Wherever His human feet may have stood last, His spirit was on the threshold of heaven as He uttered these sentences, standing as the divine High Priest on the very borders of the inner sanctuary, hard by the veil that was just about to be rent in twain by His dying agony.

### *11. THE PARTING PRAYER (John 17).*

a. Christ's prayer, as it respects Himself (17:1-5).

(1) The crisis hour. "Father, the hour is come" (17:1). It was the hour of the world's destiny, the Father's glory, and His own consummated work. Not only was His work done, but it was all done on time. Each moment had been filled with the Father's perfect will, and now there was nothing to do but to die.

Oh that we might all follow Him, not only in the faithfulness, but in the timeliness of His finished life.

(2) The finished work.

"As thou hast given him power over all flesh, that he should give eternal life to as many as thou hast given him. . . . I have glorified thee on the earth: I have finished the work which thou gavest me to do" (17:2, 4). He recalls His mighty commission to give eternal life to His people through the knowledge of the Father and the Son, and acknowledges publicly the complete resources which the Father has supplied for this mighty task. "Thou hast given him power over all flesh" (17:2) that He might thus administer the great work of salvation.

What an unfolding of the purpose and glory of redemption—Christ its mighty administrator, the whole human family its beneficiaries, His own people His especial objects and eternal life its glorious aim. And this eternal life is not a definite future existence but is a relation of intimacy and love with God. It is God Himself through Jesus Christ revealed in the soul.

This mighty task, He declares, He had fully accomplished. He has revealed the Father, He has made known His word and stood among men as His Representative and Expression. He has so done this as to glorify His Father on the earth. Not only has He fulfilled His work, but He has fulfilled it for the glory of God. What a pattern to all His followers—a finished task, and God supremely glorified. Oh! that it may be ours to echo it.

(3) The last request.

"Glorify thou me with thine own self with the glory which I had with thee before the world was. . . . Glorify thy Son, that thy Son also may glorify thee" (17:5, 1). He asks that He may be glorified and raised up from the depths of shame and sorrow to which He is about to stoop. He asks back again, as His right, the glory which, for a little while, He had voluntarily laid aside; the glory He had with the Father before the world was. He asks still more the joy of His Father's heavenly fellowship. "With thine own self" (17:5); it is the cry of the lonely heart to be again upon the Father's bosom.

How poorly can we understand that loneliness and that love of His great heart. He had said a little before, "If ye loved me, ye would rejoice, because I said, I go to My Father" (14:28). But, even then, He did not ask for Himself; still, His true heart turns instinctively to His Father's glory. He hallows even this holy prayer by the added request, "That thy Son may glorify thee" (17:1).

b. The prayer of Christ with respect to His immediate disciples (17:6-19).

(1) He commends them to His Father and tells Him:

(a) That they have been given Him by the Father Himself (17:6).

(b) That they have kept His word.

(c) That they have received the messages of the Son, knowing surely that He came from God and believing in Him with all their hearts. And in Him they have also recognized the Father and "known that all things whatsoever thou hast given me are of Thee" (17:7).

(2) He pleads for them on the ground that they are already His Father's and also His own, and that His glory is linked with their blessing. "They are thine . . . and thine are mine; and I am glorified in them" (17:9-10).

(3) He refers to His own care and keeping of them hitherto and commits them from His hands, as He is now about to leave them to His Father's keeping, telling Him that they are all safe, except the one who has wrecked himself, as the Scriptures had already predicted, the wicked son of perdition.

> While I was with them in the world, I kept them in thy name . . . and none of them is lost, but the son of perdition; that the scripture might be fulfilled. . . . And now I am no more in the world, but these are in the world, and I come to thee. Holy Father, keep through thine own name those whom thou hast given me, that they may be one, as we are. (17:12, 11)

(4) He refers to their lonely, bereaved and perilous situation, left in the world without Him and hated by the world for His sake. "The world hath hated them, because they are not of the world, even as I am not of the world" (17:14).

(5) He speaks of His desire for them that they may have His joy fulfilled in themselves.

(6) He prays for their preservation in the world, and from the evil one (17:15).

He would not have them withdrawn from the world by death, for the world needs them and they need to finish their work; but He does ask that while remaining in the world they may be preserved from evil, or, as the words more correctly read, from the evil one, and all his malignant power, both upon their souls and bodies.

(7) He asks for their sanctification, including their separation from the world (17:16), and their purification and dedication to God through the truth (17:17).

(8) He claims for them the same service as He Himself has done and sets them apart in His Father's presence to represent Him and finish His work, with the same authority which the Father hath given to Him. "As thou hast sent me into the world, even so have I also sent them into the world" (17:18).

(9) He solemnly consecrates Himself to them for their sanctification, service and complete salvation. He lays Himself with them in His death, a living sacrifice upon the altar of His Father's will, so that their sanctification does not depend upon their own personal strength and resources but is pledged by His own love to them and His own life in them.

We think of our consecration as we lay ourselves upon the altar. Let us rather think of that other Sacrifice who lies down beside us and becomes by His own consecration with us, the strength and the security of our sanctity and service. "For their sakes I consecrate myself, that they also may be truly consecrated" (17:19, author's paraphrase).

c. Christ's prayer, as it respects believers throughout the whole Christian age (17:20-24).

From the little band that are kneeling close to Him, His vision expands until He sees the whole circle of His redeemed, each one of us personally. Then He adds this all-comprehensive prayer, "Neither pray I for these alone, but for them also which shall believe on me through their word" (17:20).

The simple condition which includes us in His prayer is that we believe on Him through their word. If we can meet this, the Master's prayer has been offered for us and will surely be fulfilled, if we will let it. And this prayer not only looks forward to the words which follow, but back also to the words which He has just expressed for the eleven disciples.

Three things He asks for them in the coming ages, and one bequest He bestows upon them.

First, their unity with each other; "that they all may be one" (17:21).

Secondly, their union with Him, "I in Thee and Thou in Me;

that they also may be one in us" (17:21, author's paraphrase).

And, thirdly, the perfecting of each one of them in their personal life and of the whole body in the one complete Church—the Bride of the Lamb, "that they may be made perfect in one" (17:23). This is also the apostle's prayer, as he echoes the Master's thought: "Till we all come in the unity of the faith, and of the knowledge of the Son of God, unto a perfect man, unto the measure of the stature of the fullness of Christ" (Ephesians 4:13).

This complete unity, He tells the Father, is to be the great evidence through which the world will believe that the Father hath sent Him and will know that He has loved them even as Himself. Christian unity must have its deeper root in divine union, and Christian perfection can only come through such union between the soul and God. There is no self-perfection, but as God has revealed and ministered to each one of us, and together so united us in Him, we shall be "made perfect in one" (John 17:23). Perfection here includes, not only the completeness and maturity of individual character but also of the Church, as a collective body, at the coming of the Lord.

There is still a deeper, sweeter thought lying in the bosom of His precious words, and not yet expressed in this analysis. The issue of this divine union with the Father and the Son shall be that the soul thus linked with God shall enter into the same love which the Father has toward the Son. If Jesus be truly formed in us, the Father will love us in Jesus and as Jesus Himself. These are the two sublime heights in this prayer, so far as we are concerned—the love of Jesus and the love of the Father revealed in us through our union with God.

From this great thought naturally follows the remaining prayer (17:22-24) which contains His last bequests to His beloved followers. At the table He had bequeathed to them His peace, and now He adds to it His glory, too. All the riches, all the splendor of the infinite and everlasting wealth of His throne and His glory, He shares with them; empties Himself of all but love, and finds His sole inheritance in them and in His Father. "The glory which thou gavest me I have given them; that they may be one, even as we are one" (17:22).

And as though to complete even the very form of a will and

claim for them, by every right of His Sonship, this glorious consummation, He adds, "Father, I *will* that they also, whom thou hast given me, be with me where I am; that they may behold my glory, which thou hast given me: for thou lovest me before the foundation of the world" (17:24, emphasis added).

d. Christ's prayer as it respects His Father.

The closing thoughts and words have reference to the highest of all thoughts and themes.

(1) The Father and the world (17:25-26).

Apart from Christ, the world has no God. Man's conceptions of the Father are all distorted and false. Jesus alone has revealed Him. "No man hath seen God at any time; the only begotten Son, which is in the bosom of the Father, he hath declared him" (1:18). The altars of false religion are dedicated "to the unknown God" but "This is life eternal, that they might know thee the only true God, and Jesus Christ, whom thou hast sent" (17:3). Nothing is more pathetic than the groping of lofty minds in every age to find out God. Yes, it is true as Christ said, "The world hath not known thee" (17:25).

(2) The Father and the Son.

"These have known that thou hast sent me. And I have declared unto them thy name" (17:25-26). Jesus is the revelation of God to the world and to the believer, and only as we receive Him can we know God and enter into union with Him through Jesus Christ. When we receive His Son, we at once pass into direct and personal acquaintance with the Father. This was the very purpose of His coming "to bring us to God," and one with Him, we become one with the Father also.

(3) The Father and the Believer.

Receiving Christ and through Him united to God, there comes to us the stupendous blessing expressed in these words "that the love wherewith thou hast loved me may be in them" (17:26). We become the objects of the very same love which the Father has for His Son. We are recognized as part of Him even as the bride is taken into her husband's family and loved even as her husband. This is, indeed, the mystery of mysteries: that we are permitted to share the intimate and exclusive affection of the eternal Father toward His only begotten Son. He loves us now, not for ourselves, nor in proportion to our personal claims upon His affection, but precisely as He loves Jesus Christ, with infinite complacency and unlimited measure.

The secret of all this is expressed in the last three words of this sublime prayer, "I in them" (17:26). This is the mystery hid from ages, and at last made known to the saints. "Christ in you, the hope of glory" (Colossians 1:27).

"I in them." This explains why God can love us even as He loves His Son, for to the Father we are accepted and counted as sharing His peculiar sonship "even as He."

Even the Master's prayer cannot go higher or deeper than this. The curtain falls upon these parting words. Henceforth their echoes keep forever sounding through the ages as the very voices of the ministry of His intercession within the veil and the acknowledgement forever of our high place of unity and fellowship with Him as we, in His name, may come, and come boldly, to the throne of grace.

> So near, so very near to God,
>     More near I cannot be;
> For in the Person of His Son
>     I am as near as He.
> So dear, so very dear to God,
>     More dear I cannot be;
> The love wherewith He loves His Son,
>     That love He bears to me.